THE BLACK FRONTIERSMEN

THE JOHN DAY COMPANY · NEW YORK

THE BLACK FRONTIERSMEN

Adventures of Negroes Among American Indians 1528-1918

J. NORMAN HEARD

Library of Congress Catalogue Card Number: 79-89317

Printed in the United States of America

Designed by The Etheredges

CONTENTS

FOREWORD

In 1928 an anthropologist named Melville J. Herskovits made a startling discovery. In interviewing and examining 1,551 Negroes at Howard University, in Harlem, and in rural West Virginia, he learned to his amazement that more than one-fourth of them were partially of American Indian ancestry. Obviously the association of the red-skinned and the dark-skinned races in America has been of long duration, but it is an aspect of our cultural history which has been almost entirely neglected.

Thousands of books have been written about white frontiersmen who blazed the Wilderness Trail to the dark and bloody ground of Kentucky or corralled their wagons and stood off the attacks of wild-riding Sioux or Comanches on the Great 7

Plains. Young people for generations have relived the times of such frontiersmen as Daniel Boone, Lewis and Clark, and Kit Carson through biographical or fictional accounts of their adventures. Today's armchair adventurers spend countless hours watching exaggerated exploits of explorers and pioneers on motion-picture and television screens. It seems that the story of the white man among redskins will never satisfy the public demand.

But the part of the picture which describes the accomplishments of Negroes on the frontier has never been adequately presented. In the thick of the conflict between white men and red, many black men played important roles. A Negro named York trudged every weary mile across the continent with Lewis and Clark, Ed Rose was no less courageous than Kit Carson among the Plains Indians and the trappers of the Rocky Mountains, and a slave called Pompey was felled from the fork of a tree with a 180-yard shot by Daniel Boone as he urged his Shawnee brothers to intensify their bombardment of Boonesboro. That these men are unknown today is due to the fact that black people, by and large, have been ignored by chroniclers of the New World drama.

The full story of the Negro on the frontier deserves to be told, and one of the purposes of this book is to break a trail in that direction by bringing together some of the more thrilling adventures of black men among hostile Indian tribes. A surprising number of frontiersmen wrote accounts of their adventures or had them "ghostwritten," much as is the practice among athletes and other folk heroes of today. Their stirring narratives of wilderness warfare and capture by Indians are presented here in their own words whenever possible. When the adventurer could not or did not write his story, it is told in the words of witnesses. Beginning with Estevanico, the first

Negro in America whose name definitely is known to history,

and closing with Henry Flipper, a cavalry officer who lived until 1940, the collection of narratives spans four centuries.

The amazing adventures of Estevanico are known to many students of Western history. But the second man represented in this collection, a New England slave and Florida captive named Briton Hammon, has been forgotten in spite of the fact that he probably was the earliest American Negro author. Some of these black adventurers fought beside Indians against whites, others helped white frontiersmen conquer the Indians, and at least two were leaders in warfare between Indian tribes. Ranging in roles from a Methodist missionary to a Crow Indian chief, each of the ten men whose experiences are related in this book had at least two traits in common—an adventurous spirit and an abundance of courage.

RED MEN AND BLACK ON THE AMERICAN FRONTIER

Some historians believe that a Negro sailed to the New World with Columbus on his first voyage. It is certain that slaves were brought to this hemisphere by Spanish ships less than ten years after its discovery. In the English colonies, according to Captain John Smith, slaves were introduced in 1619 by a Dutch man-of-war.

The first Negroes encountered by Indians in the present United States were slaves of explorers. One of the earliest of these was Estevanico, a Moor who sailed from Cuba with the Narváez expedition in 1528, was cast away on the Texas coast, and made his way across deserts and mountains to the Pacific coast of Mexico. Later Estevanico discovered Arizona and entered New Mexico in search of the fabled Seven Cities of

Cíbola. When he reached Zuñi, he demanded tribute of the usually peaceful Pueblo Indians, and they snuffed out his life with a volley of arrows. A rocky beginning, indeed, of relations between red men and black!

The first meeting between Indians and Negroes in the Pacific Northwest likewise ended in tragedy. On August 16, 1788, a boatload of sailors from the ship *Lady Washington* went ashore at Tillamook Bay, in search of provisions. Marcos López, a Negro Cape Verde Islander, leaped from the boat, thrust the point of his cutlass into the sand, and strode along the beach. Hearing a rustle of running feet, he turned and dashed in pursuit of an Indian who was making off with his weapon. The red man raced toward the forest fringe with López gaining at every stride. Suddenly he leaped over a pile of driftwood, just as a swarm of Indians rose up from concealment behind some low dunes. Surrounded by menacing figures, López skidded to a halt. Then, with scarcely an outcry, he sank to the sands, his body convulsing from the impact of a dozen arrows.

One might assume from the fates of Estevanico and López that Indians hated and slaughtered Negroes at first sight, and some writers actually have concluded that red men instinctively considered themselves superior to men with black skins. On the Atlantic coast, however, the first meetings of Negroes and Indians had entirely different reactions. In 1634 three New England Indians caught sight of a black man in the top of a tree. This fearsome figure was a lost slave trying to find his way home, but the superstitious natives fled in terror to the nearest plantation to plead with the white men "to conjure the devil to his own place." In Virginia, too, Indians feared the first Negroes as a "true breed of devils."

With the possible exception of Estevanico, the Negro who was first of his race to encounter the greatest number of Indian tribes was York of the Lewis and Clark Expedition. This giant was a source of amazement to Indians, who came from great distances to see his feats of strength and to try to "wash off the paint." York was an asset to the expedition in creating goodwill between Indians and whites. He was considered "good medicine," and the Indians tried to save something of him by having their women consort with him.

What general conclusion can one reach regarding reactions of Indians upon first encountering Negroes? It would seem that the red man's reaction was one of curiosity, mingled with superstition and fear. Negro slaves, of course, had been told about Indians by their white masters, and their reactions on first seeing a red man were influenced by whatever they had heard. Since white men, with good reason, were wary of hostile Indians, it seems certain that their defenseless slaves would regard Indians with terror. They were not so terrified, however, as to be unable to act coolly in a crisis. Even a thirteen-year-old boy who was captured by Comanches (the first Indians he had ever seen) showed such bravery that he was given weapons and adopted into the tribe. At the first opportunity the boy, whose name was Jack Hardy, escaped and reached home safely.

Contrasting with the belief that Negroes and Indians were instinctive enemies is the theory that a bond of friendship between the two races developed almost immediately. Much evidence exists that such a feeling of common cause did develop in time, but Indians were friendly toward white people, too, in the beginning and did not become hostile until the Europeans' hunger for land and slaves began to alarm them. The cause which forged a bond between black men and red was exploitation by white men.

The fact that English colonists in America, North and South, owned Negro slaves is well known, but few students realize that Indians suffered the same fate. During the New England Indian wars, vanquished tribesmen frequently were

sold into slavery. Even during times of peace, Indians were

lured aboard ships and kidnapped for sale in distant colonies. It soon became known, however, that Indians were unsuited to backbreaking plantation labor. Warriors were not workers, and in Indian villages farming had been the duty of squaws.

When it was realized that Negroes made better workers than Indians, slave ships brought black people from Africa by the thousands. Then, in slave quarters, Negroes and Indians became well acquainted for the first time. In New England both races were held in subjugation, and red men and black men met on terms of equality. It is not surprising that much inter-marriage resulted. By 1730 Negro slaves in Connecticut were more numerous than Indians, and a great many men could claim ancestry in both races. In 1790 Massachusetts Negroes numbered 4,000, and there were half as many of mixed Negro and Indian parentage. Many of them lived along the coast, especially at Cape Cod and Martha's Vineyard. While the number of Negro slaves increased, Indians were killed or driven from New England until remaining red men were ab-sorbed gradually into the more adaptable races from Africa.

On the South Atlantic coast the situation was much the same. As the tribes were crushed by the whites, the surviving Indians intermarried with Negroes until they lost their identity. But in the inland South, where Indian tribes maintained their power for a century and Negro slavery prevailed even longer, Indian-Negro relationships followed a very different course. The Cherokees, Chickasaws, Choctaws, Creeks, and Seminoles (known as the Five Civilized Tribes) were too strong to en-slave, and they became slaveholders themselves. Early in Colo-nial times many white traders married Indian women and gained positions of leadership in the tribes. They introduced the ways of the white man into Indian life, among them being the institution of Negro slavery. In South Carolina, Indians held Negroes in slavery as early as 1748.

But these five powerful tribes did not treat Negro slaves **13** the same way. The Cherokees, who held more than 1,000 slaves before their removal to the Indian Territory, were such lenient masters that Negroes frequently ran away from white plantations to live with them. On the other hand, the Choctaws and Chickasaws were severe masters.

The form of slavery practiced by the Creeks and their offshoot, the Seminoles, differed greatly from that of the other Civilized Tribes. The Creeks intermarried frequently with their slaves and treated children of their Negro wives the same as their full-blood Indian children. The Seminoles were on even better terms with their slaves. In fact, black people probably were better treated by these Florida swamp dwellers than by any other tribe. Learning that safety and a warm welcome awaited them among the Seminoles, slaves began escaping to them as early as 1738. These runaways, known as Maroons, seldom were enslaved by the Seminoles. By 1838 it was estimated that 1,400 Negroes lived among the Seminoles and that only 200 of them were slaves. Even the slaves were treated as near equals, and except for contributing a small share of their corn crops to their masters, they lived much like members of the tribe.

Negroes among the Seminoles, slave as well as free, held great influence over the tribe. Through their knowledge of white men's ways they rendered valuable service to the Indians as translators and advisers when treaties were negotiated. Their greatest leader was a runaway slave from Pensacola named Abraham. He accompanied his master, Chief Micanopy, to Washington to discuss affairs of state. His services were so valuable that they won him his freedom and he became a leader in the Second Seminole War and in tribal affairs after removal to the Indian Territory (in what is now Oklahoma).

The two Seminole Wars pitted the entire might of the United States Army against scattered bands of Indians and their

Negro allies. The first of these wars broke out when the Indians stood by their Negro friends after white men invaded Florida on slave-hunting expeditions. The second war resulted from the Seminoles' refusal to remove from Florida. Their determination to fight was strengthened by the influence of Negroes who realized that surrender meant loss of freedom. During this seven-year conflict, probably the most costly of all Indian wars, Negroes fought side by side with the Seminoles and proved themselves to be courageous warriors.

After their removal to the Indian Territory the Five Civilized Tribes retained the institution of slavery. Choctaws and Chickasaws of mixed Indian and white blood established large plantations which were worked by Negro slaves. Most white men who held government or church positions in the Indian Territory favored slavery and tried to prevent Negroes from escaping to freedom in the North or in Mexico. Typical of these men was George Butler, United States agent for the Cherokees, who credited the tribe's remarkable progress to their status as slaveholders, asserting that slavery was "an incentive to any industrial pursuit."

In the Far West there were comparatively few Negroes during frontier times, and except in Texas and the Indian Territory, slavery was a minor factor. Most of them were servants of explorers, traders, or Army officers. Scarcely a one was a runaway slave, for the attractions of Florida or Mexico were much greater than the cold climate of the Western plains and mountains. A few were free Negroes who preferred the wild life of the Indian to the white man's civilization. Some of these rose to positions of power, and at least two of them became chiefs of the Crow Nation. Both men, Edward Rose and Jim Beckwourth, had several Indian wives, chosen from the tribe's leading families. But these were exceptional cases, and there was little intermarriage between Western Indians and Negroes until after the tribes had been moved onto reservations.

While black men enjoyed friendly relations with the **15**

Indians of the Northern Plains, they were regarded with contempt by some Southern Plains tribes. Probably no tribe in America enjoyed warfare against Negroes more than did the Comanches of Texas and the Indian Territory. Captain Randolph B. Marcy reported in 1850 that he had seen two small Negro girls who were the only survivors of a party massacred by Comanches while traveling from the Seminole Nation in the Indian Territory across Texas to freedom in Mexico. The Comanches had mutilated the girls' bodies with coals of fire and had cut away sections of their skin, apparently to see whether the flesh was the same as that of other races. When Marcy asked the Comanches why they had massacred the black people, he did not believe the reply that "they felt sorry for slaves and did them a favor by putting them out of their misery."

Comanches and their allies, the Kiowas, killed hundreds of Negroes in Texas. Few frontiersmen suffered more at their hands than a black rancher named Britton Johnson. A former slave, Johnson had worked hard all his life. He had a tremendously muscular physique and was famous for feats of physical strength. Moreover, he was a brave man and a crack shot, and both qualities were needed to raise a family in West Texas during the Civil War, a period in which the Comanches drove most frontier settlers back almost to Fort Worth and Austin.

In 1864, while Johnson was away from home with the herd, a Comanche war party struck the little settlement, killing one of his sons and several neighbors. Mrs. Johnson and their three other children were carried into captivity. As was their usual procedure, the Comanches tied the captives on the backs of wild horses and made a rapid retreat toward their village far out on the Staked Plain, where it was almost impossible for pursuers to find them. But Britton Johnson was no ordinary tracker. As soon as he discovered the tragedy, he buried his son and took the trail. He was not far behind the Comanches when they entered their village, and boldly he rode right up to the chief's lodge and asked permission to join the tribe. The Comanches were impressed by his cool courage, the qualities they sought when adopting captives considered to be warrior material. They took him in, and he seized the first opportunity to escape, accompanied by his family and several white prisoners.

Still the Comanches were not done with tormenting Britton Johnson. Seven years later they attacked him while, with two other Negroes, he was hauling freight across the plains. Johnson did not panic. Coolly, he ordered his men to shoot their own horses to use as breastworks. Then a desperate battle began between three black men and twenty-five Indians who circled around the little group, clinging to the sides of their ponies and exposing only one arm and leg while firing under the necks of their mounts.

Finally, Johnson's companions were killed. He stacked their rifles near him and amazed the Indians with his ability to keep up a rapid fire. Charge after charge was repulsed until finally a warrior rode right over him and ended his life with a thrust of the lance.

The Indians mutilated the three Negro bodies but threw away the scalps "as the hair was too short to be of value." When a cowboy came on the scene of the battle several days later, he found 173 empty cartridges surrounding the body of Britton Johnson.

There are several possible explanations of Comanche hostility to Negroes. Perhaps the prejudice of white Texans was known to them and, like the Indians of the Deep South, they followed the white man's lead in the matter. Another possibility was the profit motive. The Comanches were the first Indians to develop the practice of kidnapping settlers for ransom, and they found it easy to sell Negro captives to slave traders in Arkansas and the Indian Territory. Perhaps the best explanation lies in the fact that the Comanches attempted to head off all **17**

Negroes en route to Mexico to join Juan Caballo (John Horse), whose father was a Seminole and mother a Negro. The Seminoles and Negroes who had found freedom in Mexico served as a buffer between Mexicans and hostile Indians, and they fought many battles with Comanche raiders.

Finally, it has been suggested that to wild Indians, Negroes were merely "black white men" and that, as such, they were enemies to an equal extent. This theory breaks down, however, when one considers the fact that the Comanches killed every white man above the age of fifteen who fell into their hands while they sometimes adopted black men into the tribe. As one example, when Comanches attacked a party of buffalo hunters at Adobe Walls in the Texas Panhandle, their charges were directed by a Negro bugler. This black man, probably a former cavalryman, gave a good account of himself until shot off his horse by the unerring marksmen behind the walls.

While Indian reservations served as melting pots for the Negro and Indian races, communities of peoples containing white, Negro, and Indian blood developed in the mountains, swamps, and other lands too poor to be coveted by white men of means. One such community was composed of people called the Croatan Indians. These Carolina residents were regarded as "free persons of color" until 1885, when someone pointed out that the lost Englishmen of Sir Walter Raleigh's Roanoke Island colony were believed to have been absorbed by the Croatan tribe. Hastily the North Carolina legislature passed a law forbidding them to continue marrying Negroes so that the blood of Englishmen of Queen Elizabeth's time would be no further contaminated!

In consideration of the relationships of Indians and Negroes in the early days of our history one fact clearly emerges. An Indian's attitude toward a Negro was greatly influenced by the opinions of the nearest white people. Where Indians absorbed many elements of the white man's civilization, as among the powerful tribes of the South, they regarded Negroes as inferiors and sought to enslave them. On the other hand, where white men placed both Negroes and Indians on the level of slaves, much intermarriage resulted. Among those of Negro-Indian ancestry were such famous men as Crispus Attucks, called the first martyr of American liberty for his death during the Boston Massacre, and Frederick Douglass, whose efforts finally gained for Negroes the right to fight for their freedom during the Civil War.

The role which Negroes played in the Indian wars has been ignored by most frontier historians. Few students know that slaves gave their lives in defense of their masters during the early New England Indian raids. The Reverend John Williams kept slaves, and in 1704, when Canadian Indians attacked Deerfield, Massachusetts, these black people defended his home until the savages battered their way inside and overwhelmed them. Parthena, a Negro woman, was killed during the attack. After all resistance at Deerfield was ended, the Indians murdered Parthena's husband before marching the white captives off on the trail to Canada.

The annals of frontier history reveal many forgotten incidents of slaves' saving their masters' families during Indian attacks. In Kentucky an aged and crippled Negro defended a white family with great valor during a raid while his master was away. A band of Shawnees rushed the cabin, and one warrior forced his way inside before the white woman could close the door. The old slave grappled with his powerful enemy and threw him to the floor. Before the Indian could scramble to his feet, the Negro split his skull open with an ax. Then he coolly suggested to the frightened woman that she open the door just wide enough to let in one warrior at a time so that he could wipe out the entire raiding party with the ax. But the **19**

Indians had had enough. They disappeared into the wilderness from whence they had come.

A half century later a Negro boy saved the children of a white family during a Comanche raid in Texas. In 1835 a war party attacked the Peter Mercer family on the San Gabriel River. Mercer was killed. His wife and the young slave escaped by swimming the river. Mrs. Mercer then tied a grapevine around the Negro boy's waist, and he returned to rescue the frantic Mercer children. Time after time he swam the San Gabriel, each time towing a child to safety until all had made their escape.

A Texas slave named Tom won his freedom by defending his master from marauding Apaches. While prospecting, the white man was wounded. Helplessly, he watched while Tom stood off the attackers. Then the black man carried his master 30 miles to safety.

During many Indian wars, Negroes were called on to serve as fighting men in white armies. One of the first of these was the Yamassee War of 1715, fought by the colonists against a tribal alliance led by "Emperor" Brims of the Lower Creek Indians. When 70 whites and 40 Negroes were killed by the raiders, South Carolina officials organized an impromptu army of 100 white men and 100 Negroes and friendly Indians. This thoroughly integrated force hit the hostiles hard and stemmed the invasion.

In the South, white men weighed their need for additional fighting men to guard against Indian attacks against their fears of a slave uprising. In 1729 the Chickasaw Indians incited the Banbara Negroes of New Orleans to rebel. The plantation owners discovered the plan and put the Banbaras to death. This threatened uprising did not prevent the governor of Louisiana from sending slaves to wipe out a Couchas Indian village near New Orleans the same year.

Also in 1729, the Natchez Indians massacred the French

planters at Natchez but spared the lives of their slaves. Quickly an army of whites and Negroes was organized to attack the hostiles. The Natchez promised freedom to their Negro captives if they would fight against the French, and a battle developed between forces of Negroes, with whites and Indians urging them on. The slaves who fought for the French were the victors. Three of the Negroes who defended the Natchez were turned over by the French to some Tcheti Indians to be put to the torture.

While the Negroes in Louisiana developed a fear of the Indians, those in the British colonies frequently ran away to live with the tribes. In the Carolinas and Georgia, escaped slaves were armed by Indians to fight against their former masters. At the same time, white men employed other Indians, usually Catawbas, to recapture runaway slaves hiding in swamps.

In Alabama and West Florida, Negroes were victims of some of the bloodiest battles in frontier history. One of these was fought on August 30, 1813, at Fort Mims, Alabama. The Creeks, or Red Sticks, were raiding throughout the country, and 553 soldiers, white refugees, and Negro slaves gathered at a plantation, which they hastily fortified with pickets and blockhouses. The Red Sticks were led by William Weatherford, the son of a white planter and a Creek mother. Undetected, they formed a cordon around Fort Mims. Two Negro slaves tending cattle in nearby woods saw the raiders and rushed inside to give the alarm. But no one believed them, and they were flogged for telling a lie!

"Fletcher's Negro was tied up and the lash about to be applied to his back; the officers were preparing to dine; the soldiers were reposing on the ground; some of the settlers were playing cards; the girls and young men were dancing, while a hundred thoughtless and happy children sported from door to door," wrote an Alabama historian. "At that awful moment **21** one thousand Creek warriors, extended flat upon the ground in a thick ravine, thirsted for American blood."

At high noon the Creeks suddenly burst from their hiding place and rushed for the open gate. An officer tried to close it but found the way blocked by an accumulation of sand. The warriors tomahawked him and poured inside the pickets before the soldiers could mount a defense. A slaughter commenced, and the terrified defenders fled like sheep into a single crowded building. There they were herded together too closely to defend themselves.

A slave who survived the ensuing massacre reported that he was in the building when an Indian called to him: "Come out, the Master of Breath has ordered us not to kill any but white people and half-breeds." He did, and saved his life. Shortly afterward the Indians set fire to the building. An officer chopped a hole in the pickets in the hope of opening an avenue of escape to the woods. A soldier was first to make the attempt, but the Indians instantly riddled his body with bullets. White men who had been jostling to reach the escape hole quickly drew back. Then Hester, a Negro slave woman, dashed through the opening into a hail of gunfire.

Down she went, writhing with a severe wound in the breast. But the courage of desperation assisted her to scramble up and run for her life. She evaded the Red Sticks, hid in the woods until dark, and then made her way in a canoe to Fort Stoddard to give the alarm. She was one of only fourteen survivors of the Fort Mims massacre.

Another terrible tragedy involving Negroes, Indians, and whites took place in 1816 on the Apalachicola River. Florida belonged to Spain, and for many years black people had been escaping from Georgia plantations to the safety of the swamps and woodlands. Hundreds of them settled in the Apalachicola River Valley and took refuge during dangerous times in an
abandoned wooden fort which had been built by the British.

For years American plantation owners had been calling on their government to stop the flight of slaves into Spanish territory and to recover those who had already escaped. In 1790 an attempt was made to put pressure on the Creek Indians to return runaway slaves, but the powerful Creek Nation protected them instead.

One of the leaders in the movement to invade Spanish Florida was General Andrew Jackson. He regarded the Negro fort on the Apalachicola as a major obstacle, and on May 16, 1816, he wrote to General Edmund P. Gaines as follows:

"I have little doubt of the fact, that this fort has been established by some villains for the purpose of rapine and plunder, and that it ought to be blown up, regardless of the ground on which it stands; and if your mind shall have formed the same conclusion, destroy it and return the stolen Negroes and property to their rightful owners."

Two gunboats, a large force of soldiers, and some Indian allies were sent to carry out this order. On July 17 a shore party from one of the boats was ambushed near the fort by Negroes and Indians led by a black man named Garcia (also called Garcon) and a Choctaw Indian chief. As the gunboats approached the fort, the commanding officer issued a demand for surrender. The only response of the 300 defenders was to run up a blood red flag.

In an attempt to burn the bastion, the sailors heated a cannonball in the ship's galley and touched it off with devastating effect. The fiery projectile penetrated the fort's magazine, and the entire structure was shattered by a tremendous explosion. An Army officer described the ensuing scene in the following words:

The explosion was awful and the scene horrible beyond description. Our first care on arriving at the scene of destruction   **23** *was to rescue and relieve the unfortunate beings that survived the explosion.*

The war yells of the Indians, the cries and lamentations of the wounded, compelled the soldier to pause in the midst of victory, and to drop a tear for the sufferings of his fellow beings, and to acknowledge that the great ruler of the Universe must have used us as an instrument for chastising blood thirsty murderous wretches that defended the Fort. The Fort contained about one hundred effective men (including twenty five Choctaws) and about two hundred women and children. . . .

Only a handful of the Negroes and Indians survived the explosion. Garcia and the Choctaw chief were executed, and most of the others were sold into slavery.

During the Civil War the slaveholding Indians supported the Confederacy for the most part, some fighting as troops. The Cherokees were badly divided in their allegiance, and most of the other tribes wavered as the fortunes of war swung back and forth. Their slaves suffered along with them in the aftermath of destruction resulting from lands overrun by soldiers, renegades, and Indian enemies. At the end of the war the Choctaws and Chickasaws massacred some of their slaves because they blamed them for the defeat of the Confederacy.

Immediately after the Civil War the Western frontier was subjected to frequent attacks. To resist the Indians and to give employment to freedmen, two infantry (the twenty-fourth and twenty-fifth) and two cavalry (the ninth and tenth) regiments of Negroes were established in 1866. While fighting Indians throughout the West, the Negroes proved to be courageous combatants. They gained the grudging respect of the Indians, who called them Buffalo Soldiers. The Tenth Cavalry took such pride in the name that the regiment adopted the buffalo as a coat of arms.

At least fourteen Buffalo Soldiers won the Congressional

Medal of Honor. In 1875 Pompey Factor, Indian scout with the Twenty-fourth Infantry, won this coveted medal for heroism during a fight with Apaches in Texas. At the time it was believed that he was a Seminole Indian. Not until ninety years later was his identity as a Negro established.

Isaiah Dorman, a black scout who may have been part Sioux Indian, died with General George Armstrong Custer at the Battle of the Little Big Horn in 1876. The Indians spared his body when they scalped and mutilated the massacred white troopers.

In 1879, Henry Johnson, a Virginia-born black trooper of the Ninth Cavalry, won the Medal of Honor for bravery during the Battle of Milk River, in Utah. The troopers were pinned down in rifle pits by the accurate fire of the Ute Indians. Several of them were wounded and badly in need of water. Johnson, who was sergeant of the guard, led a detachment which fought its way to the Milk River and returned to the wounded with water.

Two years later, Sergeant George Jordan won the same honor for his courageous leadership of 24 Negro troopers in a battle against 100 Apaches. When a messenger brought word that the Apaches were advancing to attack Tularosa, New Mexico, Jordan and his men rode all night, reached the town ahead of the raiders, built a stockade, and stood off two Apache attacks.

At least three Buffalo Soldiers won the Medal of Honor for rescuing white officers or black troopers who were surrounded by Indians. They were Sergeant Thomas Boyne, Sergeant Moses Williams, and Private Augustus Walley.

As it is generally believed that the last battle between Indians and United States troops was fought in the nineteenth century, one of the most surprising facts about frontier warfare is that a detachment of Buffalo Soldiers had a fierce fight with Yaqui Indians from Mexico in 1918! Since the fight took place **25**

78147

at the time World War I was raging in Europe it received little attention until Cavalry Colonel H. B. Wharfield published an account of it in 1965 entitled *10th Cavalry & Border Fights*. The troop was patrolling the border near Nogales, Arizona, when suddenly the Yaquis opened fire from the crest of a ridge. While most of the Indians escaped across the border, ten warriors concealed themselves among the rocks as a rear guard and shot it out with the troopers. Finally, one of the soldiers mortally wounded the chief, and the other Indians surrendered. One of them was an eleven-year-old boy who had been firing a rifle almost as long as he was tall. The wounded chief was the boy's grandfather, and the soldiers loaded both of them into a Model T Ford and made a run for the post hospital. They had not gone far when the old Yaqui died with his head cradled in the boy's lap. Then the last and smallest warrior to fight on United States soil broke into tears. Thus Indian-Negro encounters which began when Estevanico landed on Florida sands came to a close in Arizona almost four centuries later in the back of a Model T Ford as it bounced along a dusty desert road.

Clearly, the Negro frontiersman was no coward. As a slave, he fought to defend his master. When freed, he fought to protect his own home and family from red-skinned marauders. He fought white men to preserve his freedom, he fought Indians in the service of his country, and at times he even fought other Negroes as a pawn in conflicts between Indians and whites which were none of his making. As a fighting man, he performed feats which have been almost forgotten, yet his adventures were unique, and they deserve a place in the annals of the frontier.

THE ODYSSEY OF ESTEVANICO

Estevanico was born in Azamor, Morocco, probably before 1500. Spanish soldiers captured him during an attack on that city in 1513, and he became the slave of Don Andrés Dorantes de Carranza, a nobleman of Castile. Except for his size and strength, there was little in his appearance to set him apart from other slaves. Yet his courage and ability enabled him to become the first man of African birth whose name is known to American history. A member of the first party to cross the wide part of the North American continent, he discovered Arizona and is remembered as one of the great adventurers of all time.

Estevanico sailed with his master in February, 1528, on the ill-fated expedition of Pánfilo de Narváez, northward bound from Cuba to discover, conquer, and populate the region from **27** the Rio Grande to Florida. He leaped ashore with 300 Spanish adventurers on April 7, 1528, near the spot where St. Petersburg, Florida, now stands. Advancing up the coast, he met his first Indians, the sturdy Timucuas, and marveled at golden ornaments encircling their necks and wrists. He trudged along on the first day of May, when the expedition advanced into the interior—searching for riches, but destined almost to the man to sacrifice their lives in a fruitless quest. For Estevanico it was the first leg of an eight-year journey which would span the continent, a day-by-day battle for survival against shipwreck, starvation, and Indian massacre, all the way from Florida to the Pacific coast of Mexico.

On June 25 the expedition attacked the Indian village of Apalachee. Expecting golden treasures, they found only fierce warriors who drove them away with a shower of arrows. The black man trotted beside his master's horse during a desperate retreat toward the sea, while arrows pierced Spanish armor or drove jagged points deeply into the bodies of screaming horses.

Álvar Núñez Cabeza de Vaca, the only survivor of the expedition who wrote an account of his experiences, reported that Narváez ordered the horsemen to dismount and attack the Indians on foot, but their armor failed to protect them. "There were men who swore they had seen two oak trees, each as thick as the calf of a leg, shot through and through by arrows," he reported. And he added that this feat was not surprising, for "all the Indians from Florida were archers, and being very tall and naked, at a distance they appear like giants."

At last Estevanico and his companions reached the coast at Apalachee Bay. Further retreat by land was impossible, and the desperate Spaniards, many of them sick or wounded, decided to build boats and entrust their lives to the open sea.

"God provided," recalled the devout Catholic Cabeza de Vaca, "that one of the men should come, saying that he would make wooden flues, and bellows of deerskin, and as we were in such a state that anything appearing like relief seemed acceptable, we told him to go to work, and agreed to make of our stirrups, spurs, crossbows and other implements the nails, saws and hatchets and other tools we so greatly needed for our purpose."

Forty men died, and all their horses were killed and eaten, while five of the strangest scows ever constructed were made ready for sea. Yet these clumsy craft held together while they sailed westward along the Gulf of Mexico, hoping to reach Pánuco, a Spanish outpost in Mexico. Estevanico labored in the boat commanded by his master and Captain Alonso del Castillo Maldonado, the only two survivors besides Cabeza de Vaca and himself who would ever again see a Spanish settlement. Like the white men he served, the slave had no idea of the distance between Florida and Mexico, and he shared their hope that Pánuco would be found on each point of land they sighted from Mobile Bay to Galveston Island.

The voyage ended in disaster when, in November, 1528, the boats carrying Estevanico and Cabeza de Vaca were blown ashore on La Isla de Mal Hado (Bad Luck Island) near the present Galveston, Texas. As Estevanico and his companions staggered onto the beach, they beheld a terrifying sight. A swarm of Indians appeared from concealment behind sand dunes. But no bows twanged, and no arrows pierced their skins! Instead, these strange red men took pity on them and howled in sympathy at the plight of the helpless castaways. Haughty Europeans were reduced to begging for food from a race so despised that their countrymen had fed dogs on the bodies of Indians hunted down like wild animals.

The white men owed their lives to these Indians, who fed them during a winter in which hunger took its toll of natives and Europeans alike. But a frightful change took place when some of the starving Spaniards turned to cannibalism. The Indians, Attacapas who were later to become known as man- **29** eaters, turned against them in rage. To make matters worse, a plague struck among the Spaniards, wiping out all except fifteen, and spreading to the Indians. Suspecting the white men of sorcery, the Indians forced them to cure the sick.

Cabeza de Vaca wrote that "they wanted to make medicine men of us without any examination or asking for our diplomas." The Spaniards treated the sick by breathing on them and reciting the Lord's Prayer. "Thanks to His will and the mercy He had upon us, all those for whom we prayed, as soon as we crossed them, told the others that they were cured," said Cabeza de Vaca. Estevanico became a better medicine man than did his master, Dorantes.

In April, 1529, eleven Europeans and the African, Estevanico, set out southward on foot in an attempt to reach a Spanish settlement. Cabeza de Vaca was left behind because he was too sick to travel. But Cabeza de Vaca did not die. Convinced that God would spare him for some as yet unknown purpose, he survived to become a trader and to meet again, years later, with the remnants of the group which had abandoned him, reduced by the hostilities of the Karankawa Indians to three—Dorantes, Maldonado, and Estevanico.

In the summer of 1534 these last four survivors of the Narváez expedition escaped while their masters were busy gathering the fruit of the cactus. Realizing that the coastal route was blocked by the Karankawas, they struck out westward into the mountains. Trudging from tribe to tribe, they found the Indians increasingly friendly. They cured the sick in every village, and their fame as medicine men spread as they traveled through western Texas and crossed the mountains of northern Mexico.

As they made their way westward through mountains and deserts, they were guided by friendly natives from one tribe to the next, large numbers of sorrowing Indians following and beseeching them to remain. As consolation for the loss of their marvelous medicine men, each village exacted tribute before releasing Estevanico and his companions to them. "The robbers told them that we were children of the sun, and had power to cure or kill," Cabeza de Vaca related. "They also enjoined them to treat us with great reverence and to be careful not to arouse our wrath."

Along their route the castaways received gifts of native products and one of these, a ceremonial calabash rattle, was to be a cause of Estevanico's death. In the Sonora Valley the Indians showed Estevanico a trail which crossed the mountains northward. In that direction, said the red men, lay seven large towns filled with gold and jewels.

In March, 1536, the castaways found their countrymen on the Sinaloa River. From the Gulf of Mexico to the Gulf of California, they had walked more than 3,000 miles. When they related their experiences, Spanish officials seized on the account of rich cities to the north. For four centuries a legend had been told of seven cities built on islands of golden sand. Perhaps, at last, their location was known.

The viceroy, Antonio de Mendoza, believed the story. He chose a Franciscan friar, Marcos de Niza, to lead an expedition in search of the seven cities. A guide was needed, and the viceroy purchased Estevanico from his master and directed him to obey Fray Marcos in all respects. Several Indians were freed from slavery to carry the goods which would be traded for jewels at the end of the trip.

On March 7, 1539, the red men who had regained their freedom and the black man who had merely changed masters led off along the trail which Estevanico had traveled in the opposite direction three years earlier. The procession passed through a region made desolate by drought and by Spanish slave hunters who kept the Indians too terrified to plant crops. At the Indian **31** town of Vacapa, Fray Marcos halted to rest until Easter, sending Estevanico ahead with orders to send back a large cross if he found a rich country.

And so Estevanico was on his own for the first time. No longer dependent on his former master, Dorantes, or on Cabeza de Vaca, or even on Fray Marcos, he strode northward at the head of a column of Indians, determined to make the most of his opportunity. At an Indian village he was told that the seven cities were called Cíbola and that they contained countless riches to be had for the taking. At once, Estevanico sent a messenger to Fray Marcos, carrying a cross as tall as a man.

The Opata Indians joined Estevanico's expedition, hoping to obtain a share of the spoils. Beautiful Indian maidens walked behind the conquering black man, eager to serve this amazing stranger, and warriors with bows and arrows fanned out along the trail. Striding in step with the sound of reed flutes, shell fifes, and fish-skin drums, the bearded Negro created his own music with tinkling bells which encircled his arms and legs. As the column crossed Arizona and entered New Mexico, the Zuñi Indians who watched from the mesas must have wondered from what strange land the commander came. His display of pomp and power gave no clue to his true identity. No one would have believed that Estevanico was a slave.

At last Estevanico drew near Hawikuh, a Zuñi Indian pueblo and the first of the so-called Seven Cities of Cíbola. He sent some Indians ahead, bearing the ceremonial calabash rattle which he had obtained while crossing the continent with Cabeza de Vaca. He had no way of knowing that this rattle had been given to him by Indians who were mortal enemies of the Zuñi tribe.

Soon the messengers returned with a dismaying report. The ceremonial rattle had been rejected by the Zuñi chief. "After he spied the bells, in a great rage and fury he cast it to

the ground, and told the messengers to get out of there with speed, for he knew well enough what people they were, and they should in no case enter the city, for if they did he would put them all to death."

But Estevanico refused to heed the chief's warning. Hostile Indian villages held no terrors for him. He had visited hundreds of them during his trek from sea to sea, and his powerful "medicine" had saved him every time. Had not his Opata companions told him that they traded with these mild-mannered people and took what they wanted when the Zuñis balked at their terms? The risk was small when weighed against the riches concealed in the mysterious adobe houses which towered several stories above the shifting sands. The black chieftain had no fear that his charmed life had run its course, that his blood would stain the sun-baked sand outside the Seven Cities of Cíbola.

Meanwhile, Fray Marcos was hurrying to overtake the advance party. He was still many miles behind, however, when an Indian who had been with Estevanico came running toward him. Marcos related to his superiors that this man "came in a great fright, having his face and body all covered with sweat, and showing great sadness." The news which he brought was sad indeed, for he told Marcos that he had witnessed the death of many of his companions and he believed Estevanico to have been among them.

The exhausted Indian reported that Estevanico had advanced to the edge of the city, only to find that the Zuñis would not let him enter. "They shut him into a great house which stood without the city, and took all things from him which he carried to truck and barter with them, and they kept him there all that night without giving him meat or drink." The Indian concluded his story by telling Marcos that early in the morning he had gone to the river to drink. Suddenly he had seen Estevanico and his companions running for their lives, pursued by the Zuñis. Many of them fell, riddled by arrows. **33**

Ruins at Hawaikuh, New Mexico. Here Estevanico, the first black man known to North American history, was killed by the Zuñi Indians while seeking the Seven Cities of Cibola in 1539.

(*Museum of New Mexico, Santa Fe*)

Since his informant had not actually seen Estevanico die, Marcos did not entirely abandon hope that he had survived. But soon two other Indians staggered into view, covered with blood from many wounds. Their stories agreed with the details of the first survivor's report:

When the sun was a lance high, Estevanico went out of the house, and some of the chief men went with him. Suddenly people came from the city. Estevanico began to run, and we likewise, and at once they shot and wounded us, and certain dead men fell upon us, and so we lay until night and dare not stir. And after this we could see Estevanico no more, and we think they have shot him to death, as they have done all the rest, so that none are escaped but we only.

Fray Marcos claimed that he advanced up the trail until he could see the city from the top of a hill. Then he returned to Mexico and gave glowing reports of the riches of Cíbola. When an expedition reached the city the following year, however, no riches were found, and the commander branded the entire story a lie.

But the fact remains that Estevanico was dead. If the story told to Marcos by the black man's Indian companions was a lie, perhaps we can believe a legend handed down through the centuries by the Indians who did the killing. Frank Cushing, a white man adopted into the Zuñi tribe, was told the legend of the death of the "Black Mexican":

It is to be believed that a long time ago the Black Mexicans came from their homes in Everlasting Summerland. But when they said they would enter, our ancient people looked not gently at them. For with these Black Mexicans came many Indians of Sinaloa, as they call it now, who carried war feathers and long bows and cane arrows like the Apaches, the enemies of our ancient people. Therefore our ancient people, being always bad tempered and quick to anger, rushed out of their town, shouting, skipping, and shooting with slingstones and arrows and tossing their warclubs. Then the Indians of Sinaloa set up a great howl, and they and our ancients did much ill to one another. Thus was killed a Black Mexican, a large man with chili lips.

Perhaps this legend is closer to truth than any other account of the death of this remarkable slave who will always be remembered as the discoverer of Arizona.

BRITON HAMMON RETURNS TO HIS NATIVE LAND

Briton Hammon, a Massachusetts slave, was assigned by his master, General Winslow of Marshfield, to work in the maritime trade. On Christmas Day, 1747, he signed as a hand on Captain John Howland's sloop, outward bound from Plymouth to Jamaica. Reaching the beautiful tropical island about February 1, 1748, the sloop sailed on to the bay area, where it remained until late spring, loading a logwood cargo.

On May 25 the dangerous return voyage through the Straits of Florida began. Seafaring men had dreaded this passage between Florida and the Bahama Islands for two centuries, fearing not only storms but pirates, Indians, and enemy warships as well. In the middle of the eighteenth century no voyage anywhere in the world was safe, and few were more dangerous than this. Of the eleven men on board, only Briton Hammon would ever sail again, for the sloop was doomed to add to the wreckage strewn along the Florida sands from Biscayne Bay to Cape Kennedy.

The end of the voyage came suddenly with a grinding tremor as the sloop went hard aground on a reef, five leagues from shore. "Being now destitute," said Briton Hammon, "we knew not what to do or what course to take in this our sad condition. The captain was advised, entreated, and begged, by every person on board, to heave over but 20 tons of the wood, and we should get clear. If he had done so, he might have saved his vessel and cargo, and his own life as well as the lives of the mate and nine hands."

After being aground on the reef two days, Captain Howland decided that the danger from Indians ashore was less to be dreaded than the certainty of starvation on board. He ordered the crew to move food, arms, and ammunition to the mainland. Because the lifeboat could not carry all hands with the first load, he called for volunteers to remain on board until a second trip could be made. But the entire crew was eager to leave the vessel as quickly as possible. Finally, Howland himself decided to remain on board, keeping two men. The mate with seven seamen, one of whom was Briton Hammon, set sail for the shore.

Hammon related that within two leagues of the shore:

we spied a number of canoes, which we at first took to be rocks, but soon found our mistake, for they moved toward us. We presently saw an English colour hoisted in one of the canoes, at the sight of which we were not a little rejoiced. But on advancing yet nearer, we found them, to our great surprise, to be Indians of which they were sixty. Being now so near them we could not possibly make our escape. They soon came up with us and boarded us, took away all our arms, ammunition, and **37**

provisions. The whole number of canoes (being about twenty)
then made for the sloop, except two they left to guard us, who
ordered us to follow them.

The eighteen canoes flashed through the surf, powered by warriors long accustomed to paddling in open waters. They reached the sloop three hours ahead of the black seaman and his companions. By the time the lifeboat pulled alongside, the Indians had murdered Captain Howland and the other men left aboard and were swarming all over the luckless vessel.

"We came to the larboard side of the sloop, and they ordered us round to the starboard," Hammon recalled, "and as we were passing round the bow, we saw the whole number of Indians, advancing forward and loading their guns. The mate said, 'My lads we are all dead men.' And before we got round, they discharged their small arms upon us, and killed three of our hands: Reuben Young of Cape Cod, Mate; Joseph Little and Lemuel Doty of Plymouth. I immediately jumped overboard, choosing rather to be drowned than to be killed by those barbarous and inhuman savages."

But it was not Hammon's time to die. As he swam desperately out to sea, the Indians fired another volley into the boat, and he saw the remaining five crewmen pitch lifeless into the water. Quickly the Indians made sure that all the white men were dead. Then some of them paddled after the swimming slave. Hauling Hammon into one of the canoes, the warriors beat him severely, then tied him hand and foot. As a climax to their day of destruction, they set fire to the sloop and circled around her, shouting and singing until she burned to the water's edge.

As the twenty war canoes rode the waves toward the mainland, Hammon had cause to wish that he had drowned or been shot with the others, for one of the Indians who spoke broken **38** English taunted that a special fate was in store for him—to be

Florida Indians in war canoe. Briton Hammon was captured near the Florida coast by warriors in twenty canoes. He was the only survivor when the Indians burned his ship and massacred the crew.
(*Smithsonian Institution*)

roasted alive. "But the providence of God ordered it otherwise," said the slave, and his captors kept him under guard in one of their huts.

Years later, Briton Hammon wrote an account of his adventures which probably was the first book ever published by an American Negro. He did not tell much about his treatment while held by the Indians, nor did he attempt to identify the tribe into whose hands he had fallen. But he did provide clues. The description of Indian huts, the size of canoes, the practice of plundering and burning vessels, and the fact that the tribe traded with the Spanish and hated the English—all point to the Ais people, the largest tribe along the South Atlantic coast of Florida at the time.

The Ais Indians had been allies of the Spaniards since **39**

1600, when they offered to fight against the French and English. Before that time they had had two fights with the Spanish: one for murdering two men sent by the governor to make a treaty with them and the other for harboring two Negro slaves who had escaped into the swamps and married into the tribe. About fifteen years after Hammon fell into their hands, they moved to Havana, Cuba, when Spain ceded Florida to Great Britain.

During Hammon's captivity he feared that his life hung on the whim of the chief, and it probably did. When another ship fell into the hands of the Ais, Jonathan Dickinson reported that warriors "foamed at the mouth" at the sight of the prisoners. The Dickinson castaways were finally saved by the Spanish, but several of his Negro slaves died while trying to reach safety in St. Augustine.

Briton Hammon, like Jonathan Dickinson, was saved by the Spaniards. "The way I made my escape from these villains was this," he reported:

A Spanish schooner arrived there from San Augustine. The master, whose name was Romand, asked the Indians to let me go on board his vessel, which they granted, and the captain weighed anchor and carried me off to Havana. After being there four days the Indians came after me, and insisted on having me again, as I was their prisoner. They made application to the Governor. The Governor told them that as they had put the whole crew to death, they should not have me again, and paid them ten dollars for me. He added that he would not have them kill any person hereafter, but take as many as they could of those cast away, and bring them to him, for which he would pay them ten dollars a head.

The New England Negro was thus redeemed from a life of captivity in Florida, only to learn that some form of slavery awaited him wherever he went. After his arrival in Havana he was allowed some freedom for a time. But while he was walking the streets one day, a press gang seized him for the purpose of working as a deckhand on a ship bound for Spain. When he refused to go aboard, he was thrown into a dungeon. After almost five years in prison he gained his release from confinement with the help of a Boston sea captain, but he was denied permission to leave Cuba. Three times that year he tried to escape. Once he hid on an outward-bound English ship but was discovered, and the captain put back into port and handed him over to Spanish authorities.

For a while he worked for the Bishop of Havana. He served in an eight-man crew which carried the bishop on their shoulders in a large armchair. As the church official traveled in this fashion to baptize the children and confirm the old people, Hammon saw a wide area of the island while casting about for a means of escape.

Finally, Hammon contrived, with the help of a British lieutenant, to hide on a ship named the *Beaver*. Spanish officials discovered his hiding place and demanded his return, but the captain "refused to deliver up any Englishman under English colours" and set sail for Jamaica. From the West Indies, Hammon made his way to London on board another ship. Pressed into action with the English fleet, he served on warships in fights with the French. On board the *Hercules*, a 74-gun ship, he was wounded in a major battle with a French 84-gun vessel. Too badly injured for further naval service, he was permitted in 1759 to sail on a ship bound for Boston and reunion with his master.

Perhaps it is a measure of the hardships to which he was subjected as captive of the Indians and prisoner of the Spanish to note the joy he expressed at resuming the life of a slave: "And now, that in the Providence of that God, who delivered his servant David out of the paw of the lion, I am freed from a long and dreadful captivity, and am returned to my own native land."

41

A BLACK BOY CAPTIVE OF THE CHEROKEES

John Marrant was born of free Negro parents in New York on June 15, 1755. Following the death of his father in 1759, the family moved to the Cherokee frontier in Georgia. The boy received an elementary education, and at the age of eleven he was sent to Charleston, South Carolina, to learn a trade. But John was a talented musician, and he abandoned training to spend his time playing the violin and French horn at the numerous Charleston balls.

"I was now in my thirteenth year," he recalled, "devoted to pleasure, a slave to every vice suited to my nature and to my years. One evening I was sent for to go and play for some gentlemen and on my way I saw many people going into a large meeting house where the Rev. George Whitfield was preaching. This raised my curiosity to go in, that I might hear what he was hallooing about. I was pushing the people to make room just as Mr. Whitfield was naming his text. And looking around directly at me, and pointing with his finger, he uttered these words: 'Prepare to meet thy God, O Israel.' The Lord accompanied the word with such power, that I was struck to the ground, and lay both speechless and senseless for twenty-four minutes."

This experience converted John into a dedicated servant of the Lord. When he visited his mother in Georgia, he was distressed to find that she did not share his religious convictions. Believing him mad, his brothers and sisters taunted him until he was tempted to take his own life.

Greatly disturbed, John went into the woods, carrying only a hymnbook and a pocket Bible. As soon as the dense forest closed around him, the boy became hopelessly lost. For almost a week he wandered aimlessly through the wilderness, finding nothing but deer grass to eat and becoming almost too weak to walk. Every night packs of wolves surrounded him, howling hungrily. Fear of the savage beasts enabled him to summon strength enough to scramble to safety in a tree. One evening, just at dusk, he was climbing a giant, moss-draped oak when he saw a sight more terrifying than wolves. A heavily armed Cherokee warrior stalked into the clearing and signaled to him to descend.

Expecting a stroke of the tomahawk, John found, instead, a strong arm to lean on. The friendly Indian looked after him until he regained his strength. Then he led him deeper into the wilderness on a hunting expedition. "Our employment," John related, "was killing deer and taking off their skins by day." The nights were spent in defending themselves against wolves. "We collected a number of large bushes and placed them nearly in a circle. When joined at the ends they made a green covering which provided a shelter from the weather. What moss we **43** could gather was strewed upon the ground, and this composed our bed. A fire was kindled in the front of our temporary lodging-room, and fed with fresh fuel all night, as we slept and watched by turns; and this was our defence from the dreadful animals, whose shining eyes and tremendous roar we often saw and heard during the night."

John learned the Cherokee language, as well as the ways of the wilderness, from his companion. At the end of the hunt the Indian insisted that the boy accompany him to the Cherokee village, assuring him that he would not be harmed. John was afraid of the Indians, but he chose to take his chances among them, rather than return to a family which rejected his religious beliefs.

"There was an Indian fortification all around the town," he related, "and a guard placed at each entrance. The hunter passed one of these without molestation, but I was stopped by the guard and examined. They asked me where I came from, and what was my business there? My companion of the woods attempted to speak for me but was not permitted to. I was surrounded by about 50 men, and carried to one of their chiefs. I told him I came with a hunter, whom I met in the woods. He replied, 'Did I not know, that whoever came there, without giving a better account than I did, was to be put to death?' "

The chief called an executioner and ordered him to carry out the sentence on the following afternoon. Then John was thrown into "a low dark place, very dreary and dismal," where he spent the night praying and singing.

"At the hour appointed for my execution," John said, "I was taken out and led to the destined spot, amidst a vast number of people. The executioner showed me a basket of turpentine wood, stuck full of small pieces, like skewers. He told me I was to be stripped naked, and laid down in the basket, and these sharp pegs were to be stuck into me, and then set on fire, and when they had burnt to my body, I was to be turned on the other side, and served in the same manner, and then to be taken by four men and thrown into the flame, which was to finish the execution. I burst into tears and asked what I had done to deserve so cruel a death. To this he gave no answer."

The Cherokee questioned John closely. "How did you come here?"

"I came with a hunter whom I met in the woods, and who persuaded me to come here."

"How old are you?"

"Not yet fifteen."

"How were you supported before you met this man?"

"By the Lord Jesus Christ."

"Does He live where you come from?"

"Yes. And here also."

At that moment the chief's daughter entered the lodge. A maiden of nineteen, she showed much interest in John's Bible and asked to examine it. When she returned it to John, the chief ordered him to read from it.

After John had read the fifty-third chapter of Isaiah and the twenty-sixth chapter of St. Matthew's Gospel, the chief interrupted to ask why he pronounced the name of God with such reverence.

"Because the Being to whom those names belonged made heaven and earth and you and me."

Instantly the chief's anger arose. He had not been made in any such manner!

Then John pointed to the sun. "Who made the sun and moon and stars?"

"A man in this town does it," the chief replied.

John tried without success to convince him that no Indian medicine man held such power. Then he began to pray loudly in the Cherokee language. "In the midst of the prayer," John asserted, "some of them cried out, particularly the chief's daughter. This made the chief very angry. He called me a **45** witch, and commanded that I be thrust into prison and executed the next morning."

But John Marrant was to be saved from fiery death a second time by the power of his prayers over the Indians. During the night the chief's daughter and one other Cherokee became increasingly ill. At dawn the chief summoned the captive and threatened to chop him into little pieces if he failed to make them well. The boy at once fell to his knees, and his prayers were again answered. Both sick Indians recovered. "A great change took place among the people," John recalled. "The chief's house became God's house, the guards were ordered away, and the poor condemned prisoner had perfect liberty, and was treated like a prince."

The boy remained for nine weeks with the Cherokees. Then he visited the Creek Indians and other tribes. "These nations," he reported, "were then at peace with each other, and I passed among them without danger, being recommended from one to another." After a brief return visit to the Cherokees he decided that the time had come to patch up the hard feelings with his family.

When John reached home, his appearance was so greatly changed that at first his family failed to recognize him. "My dress was purely in the Indian style," he related. "The skins of wild beasts composed my garments, my head was dressed in the savage manner, with a long pendant down my back, a sash around my middle, without breeches, and a tomahawk by my side." Soon after his disappearance a body, badly torn up by wolves, had been found and indentified as his own. Thus, when he revealed his identity, he was welcomed as one returned from the dead.

John remained with his family until the outbreak of the American Revolution thrust him again into a life of adventure. Pressed into service as a musician in the British Navy, he served

first on the *Scorpion* and later on the 84-gun *Princess Amelia*.

"I was in the siege of Charleston," he related, "and passed through many dangers. When the town was taken, the chief of the Cherokee Indians, riding into town with General Clinton, saw me and knew me. He alighted from his horse, and came to me. He said he was glad to see me and that his daughter was very happy with the religion I had taught her."

During a storm in the West Indies, John was washed overboard in shark-infested waters and thrown back on deck by the waves. Later he was wounded in a bloody naval battle with the Dutch. After a long stay in an English hospital he was released from military service.

While John remained in England, he studied religion and prepared himself to return to America as a man of God. At that time he wrote an account of his adventures which ended with the following sentence: "I have now only to entreat the earnest prayers of all my Christian friends, that I may be carried safe there; kept humble, made faithful and successful; that strangers may hear of and run to Christ; and that Indian tribes may stretch out their hands to God."

Little is known of John Marrant's later life. He became a traveling preacher and a Mason and he sometimes occupied Masonic pulpits. He probably was the first Negro minister of the Gospel in North America.

DANIEL BOONE AND THE BLACK SHAWNEE

Pompey lived and died in slavery. Little is known of his early life, but it is probable that he labored on a Virginia plantation until captured in a Shawnee Indian raid. It is possible, however, that he ran away from his white master to live with the Indians, believing that he would be better treated as a slave of the Shawnees.

There is no mention of Pompey in frontier tradition before 1778. If he joined in attacks on isolated settlers' cabins, the defenders failed to detect a black face among copper-colored raiders, or they did not live to tell the tale. British records do not show whether he herded American captives to Fort Detroit or held scalps on high and gave the war whoop to receive his reward from Lieutenant Governor Henry Hamilton during the early years of the American Revolution. Although an outstanding historian, Reuben Gold Thwaites, has called him "a fellow of some consequence among the Shawnees," he was as unknown to frontiersmen as Adam's off-ox until his fate became entwined with that of Daniel Boone during one of the most famous battles in the annals of Indian warfare. None save his last days are known, but he lived in frontier tradition as the black warrior of the siege of Boonesboro.

During the year 1778, one of the most violent in frontier history, the settlers of Kentucky learned about Pompey. Something is known of his days as a warrior because the historian Lyman C. Draper interviewed Kentucky citizens whose fathers had fought against him during the American Revolution. Dr. Draper collected all the information available about the capture of Daniel Boone and the siege of Boonesboro. These interviews, constituting a part of the Draper Manuscripts, are owned today by the Wisconsin Historical Society. Without them, Pompey would be as entirely forgotten as hundreds of other Negroes who died in the Indian wars.

It was during a blinding snowstorm in February, 1778, that Daniel Boone first encountered Pompey. Indians usually left off raiding Kentucky during the winter, and Boone felt safe in taking 30 men from his settlement, Boonesboro, to a place called Blue Licks to make the salt which was badly needed for curing and seasoning meat. But the Shawnees were so enraged over the murder by American soldiers of their great Chief Cornstalk while on a mission of peace that they took to the warpath in the dead of winter.

While his 30 woodsmen boiled salt water in immense kettles, Boone scouted the wilderness in search of game. Some six miles from camp he shot a buffalo and loaded his horse with meat. Returning to Blue Licks, he was leading his heavily burdened animal through the snow when four Shawnees leaped on him from the trunk of a huge uprooted tree. Twisting free

Old Fort at Boonesboro, Kentucky. Pompey, black warrior and interpreter of the Shawnee Indians, poured a deadly fire into this stockade from across the river until Daniel Boone shot him out of a tree during the siege of Boonesboro. This drawing was published first in Collins' History of Kentucky.

of their grasp, he made a desperate run for his life, but one of the Indians mounted Boone's own horse and rode him down.

When Boone's captors escorted him to their camp, he found himself in the hands of more than 100 Shawnees, all hideously painted. To make matters worse, among the raiders were 2 white men, brothers of Simon Girty, the "white renegade," whose very name struck terror throughout the frontier. In the pay of the British governor in Detroit, their assignment was to arouse the Shawnees to drive the settlers from Kentucky. As Boone's eyes swung around the circle of captors, they fastened in surprise on a black face. Pompey, the unknown slave, was out on a raid with his Shawnee masters.

The leader of the raid was a famous war chief named Blackfish. Delighted over Boone's capture, he led his warriors in a stately procession to shake hands with the great leader of the "long knives," as the Kentucky frontiersmen were called by the Indians. Blackfish decided at once to make an Indian of Boone and to adopt him as his son.

Pompey was pressed into service as interpreter. He told Boone for Blackfish that the Shawnees were on their way to attack Boonesboro. They had already discovered the saltmakers' camp at Blue Licks and would massacre the 30 men before advancing against the settlement. Quickly Daniel Boone devised a plan. He knew that with the loss of the saltmakers, Boonesboro would not be strong enough to stand off such a large force of Indians. The settlement had no chance unless he could persuade Blackfish to call off the attack.

Boone had been on the frontier so long that he could "think Indian." He knew the prestige enjoyed by the leader of a successful raid who returned without losing a warrior. Perhaps with 30 prisoners as proof of his prowess, Blackfish would cut short his expedition if he believed that Boonesboro's stockade was too strong to be taken.

"Tell Blackfish I will go tomorrow, myself, and persuade **51** my men at Blue Licks to surrender," he said to Pompey, "but he will have to guarantee that they will not be tortured or forced to run the gauntlet." Insisting that he favored the British and wanted his settlement to remain loyal to the king, he made Pompey and Blackfish believe that Boonesboro was too strong to be taken. But he offered to return in the spring with a much larger war party and persuade the settlers to go live in the Indian villages.

Pompey went into a huddle with Blackfish and other Indian leaders, while Boone concealed his anxiety. At last the interpreter reported that Blackfish had accepted the proposal. But before Boone could appreciate this good news, the black man announced that if the saltmakers put up a fight, all of them would be tomahawked.

Stealthily, early the next morning, the Shawnees surrounded the Blue Licks salt camp. Then, suddenly, they raised the war whoop. The startled Kentuckians scurried for cover, but Boone screamed at them to surrender or every man would pay with his scalp. Gambling their lives on the great scout's shouted assurance that they would be turned over to Governor Henry Hamilton at Detroit, they stacked their rifles and followed Pompey's orders to sit in a circle.

But not all the Indians felt bound to honor Blackfish's promise of safe conduct. Some young warriors reminded the chief of the need to avenge the murder of Cornstalk and demanded another council to decide the fate of the captives. Pompey whispered a translation to Boone, but none of the other whites realized that their lives hung by a thread as each Shawnee arose in turn and argued whether to kill them or not. They discovered their danger only when Daniel Boone arose to plead for their lives.

Brothers! What I have promised you, I can much better
fulfill in the Spring than now; then the weather will be warm,

and the children can travel from Boonesboro to the Indian towns, and all live with you as one people. You have got all the young men; to kill them, as has been suggested, would displease the Great Spirit, and then you could not expect future success in hunting nor war; and if you spare them they will make you fine warriors, and excellent hunters to kill game for your squaws and children. These young men have done you no harm; they were engaged in a peaceful occupation, and unresistingly surrendered upon my assurance that such a step was the only safe one; I consented to their capitulation on the express condition that they should be made prisoners of war and treated well; spare them, and the Great Spirit will smile upon you.

When Pompey completed the translation, Blackfish and the older Indians growled their approval of Boone's words. But the young warriors still cried for revenge, and when the vote was taken by passing a war club, 59 of them hurled it to the ground as a ballot for death. The lives of the captives were saved by a margin of two votes.

With striking success already in their grasp, the Shawnees abandoned their advance on Boonesboro and returned at once to their villages. Blackfish kept his promise to see that the captives were not tortured, and most of them eventually escaped or were ransomed. Boone was adopted into the chief's family. He pretended to be content with life as an Indian, but he waited only for the right time to escape. When he saw that the Shawnees were planning a raid, he slipped into the woods and mounted a horse. Riding the 160 miles to Boonesboro in four days, he arrived in time to warn the settlement to prepare for an Indian attack.

About ten o'clock on the morning of September 7, 1778, a war party of 440 Shawnees, Wyandots, Cherokees, Delawares, Mingos, Frenchmen, and 1 Negro emerged from the woods near the stockade. Pompey immediately strode up to the fort **53** with a flag of truce. Mounting a stump and waving his flag, he gave the long "haloo" of the frontiersman. There was no reply, for Boone was too wise to betray the weakness of the defenders by seeming too eager to parley. Then Pompey called out that he had brought dispatches from Detroit and asked Boone to come out and receive them. The scout declined and invited Pompey to bring them to the gate.

At that moment Blackfish came within hailing distance and urged "his son" Daniel to come out. Boone knew that Blackfish was a man of his word. He agreed to meet the chief at a large stump between the fort and the Indian lines. Before escorting him to Blackfish, Pompey handed Boone a present of roasted buffalo tongues for the white family which the chief still expected to make a part of his own.

Then began two days of parleys. Hoping to delay the fight until reinforcements arrived from Virginia, Boone talked at length while Pompey translated. Blackfish was content to let the councils drag on, confident that his adopted son loved him and would agree sooner or later to bring his white friends to live with his red "brothers."

During the discussions the Kentuckians put up a brave front. Attempting to convince the Indians that there was a large force in the fort, they kept women, children, and Negro slaves moving about where their heads could be seen over the stockade. Even dummies were rigged up with hats and rifles. Pompey very nearly discovered the trick, for he kept trying to get near the fort. Boone finally threatened to shoot him if he came any closer.

"It was a critical period for us," Boone reported. "We were a small number in the garrison.—A powerful army before our walls, whose appearance proclaimed inevitable death. Death was preferable to captivity. And in the evening of the ninth, I returned answer, that we were determined to defend our fort while a man was living."

Convinced at last that Boone had deceived him at Blue Licks, Blackfish tried a trick of his own. Asking for a final parley beside the Kentucky River, he planned to capture Boone and eight other whites by having two warriors shake hands with each of them "according to Indian custom," then drag them over the bank and beyond protection of the blockhouses. The scheme almost succeeded, but the Kentuckians broke from the grasps of the Indians and escaped to the fort.

Then began the longest siege in Kentucky frontier history. For eleven days the Indians fired into the fort. They tried to storm the stockade, to destroy it with fire arrows, and to blow it up by tunneling under the walls. With only about 40 fighting men in the fort, the Kentuckians were outnumbered 10 to 1. They counted heavily on their slaves for support, and the black men did not disappoint them. One of the defenders who died in action was a slave named London. One night he disappeared into the darkness to search for an Indian who had crawled up within a few yards of a break in the stockade. When the Indian fired his rifle at the men in the blockhouse, London attempted to shoot at the flash. The Indian and the black man dueled in the darkness until London's flintlock missed fire. Then the warrior shot him to death.

Among the attackers none was more aggressive than Pompey. He not only sniped at the fort, but kept taunting the men in the blockhouses and calling out demands for surrender.

The stockade was nearly shot to pieces as Pompey and his companions poured more than 125 pounds of lead into the walls. Fortunately for the defenders, showers fell heavily. Not only did the rain put out the fire arrows, but it also softened the earth and caused the Indians' tunnel to collapse.

At the end of a week the Indians became discouraged, especially after their days of backbreaking tunneling had failed. Many of them wanted to abandon the siege. But Pompey was as determined as ever. Shouldering a large long-range rifle, he **55** crossed the Kentucky River and climbed high into the branches of a giant sycamore. By sighting through a fork in the tree, he could fire over the walls without exposing his body to the deadly aim of the Kentucky marksmen. From this vantage point he killed one man and wounded another while the defenders peered into the forest attempting to locate the source of the shots.

At last Daniel Boone spotted a puff of smoke drifting from high in the sycamore. "I'll fix your flint for you," he said in his quiet manner. Then, slowly, he raised his rifle, loaded with a 1-ounce ball, and squeezed the trigger. Down tumbled Pompey, shot through the forehead at a distance of 180 yards.

After Pompey's death the Indians gave up the attack. Thirty-six red and one black warriors had paid with their lives, and the defense was as determined as ever. Abandoning the siege, the Shawnees disappeared into the forest, carrying the bodies of the dead Indians away to save their scalps from the Kentuckians. But the lifeless form of the black man remained where it had fallen at the foot of the tree.

By belittling their slave in this way, the Indians brought dishonor on themselves, for Pompey had served them well as an interpreter, and at the ordeal of Boonesboro he had proved himself to be one of their bravest warriors.

THAT RASCAL ED ROSE

Edward Rose was born near Louisville, Kentucky. Chiefly of Negro ancestry, he had traces of white and Cherokee Indian blood. The date of his birth is unknown, but he was a grown man by 1800. As a big, brawny youth he left home on a keelboat, bound for New Orleans. Along the river he became a famous fighter. Once a brawler who must have been as tough as the legendary Mike Fink bit off the tip of Ed's nose, and for many years, along the rivers and in the Rocky Mountains, the muscular black man was known as "Cut-Nose" Rose.

In the spring of 1806 Rose chanced to be in St. Louis when a party of hunters passed through on their way to the West. Always ready for a dangerous adventure, he joined up to spend the winter in Indian country along the Osage River. The following spring, Manuel Lisa, the man who made St. Louis the headquarters for the Rocky Mountain fur trade, sent a large party of trappers into the unknown Yellowstone River country. With this reckless band, the earliest of the mountain men, Ed Rose easily held his own. He impressed Lisa with his courage and was chosen to spend the winter with the Crow Indians.

Rose rode into the Crow villages with a tremendous stock of trade goods. Almost at once he became a great man in their eyes. He learned their language quickly and amazed them with his skill as a hunter, horseman, and hand-to-hand fighter. On buffalo hunts he made the largest number of kills, and in warfare against their Blackfoot Indian enemies he was out in front in every charge.

Rose was more than generous with his Indian friends, giving them goods which his employer had intended to be traded for furs. When he returned to the post on the Yellowstone with few beaver skins, Manuel Lisa gave him a tongue lashing. Had Lisa known Rose better, he would have held his temper, for his rash words almost cost him his life. Rose would have killed him if another trapper, John Potts, had not intervened.

While Rose and Potts were scuffling, Lisa ran from the room and went on board one of his boats which was just leaving the shore. Rose saw his intended victim escaping. Livid with rage, he ran to a swivel gun, swung it to bear on the boat, and touched it off with his pipe. Just at that moment a man was passing in front of its muzzle. Fortunately, he was long-limbed, so that all the bullets passed harmlessly between his legs. He leaped into the air and fell in a heap in front of the gun, screaming that he had been killed.

The boat crew was equally fortunate. The men were seated on benches, and they could have been safe in no other place, for every shot went through the cargo box in a raking line. Rose

immediately began recharging the gun, but fifteen trappers

Crow Indian Mud Dance. Ed Rose, black chief of the Crow Nation, was a famous dancer and warrior. He was one of the first trappers to penetrate the Rocky Mountains.

(*Library, State Historical Society of Colorado*)

wrestled him to the ground, allowing Lisa to make good his escape.

Not long after this incident, Rose leaped on his horse and lashed him out of camp. Fed up with white man's ways, he rode back to the Crow camp to resume his life as an Indian.

Rose lived for a year with the Crows, a Plains tribe which was famous for horse stealing and buffalo hunting. Then he moved in with the Arikaras, who lived in fortified towns on the Missouri River. He was with the Arikaras in 1809, when Andrew Henry and a party of trappers hired him as guide and interpreter. They crossed the Rocky Mountains and spent the winter on the Snake River in Idaho.

The next spring Rose returned to the Crows, soon to become a chief as a result of his exploits against the tribe's enemies. Captain Reuben Holmes, an Army officer who met Rose in the mountains, published an account of the black man's adventures which made him famous in St. Louis and throughout the West:

> *Rose possessed qualities, physical and mental, that soon gained him the respect of the Indians. He loved fighting for its own sake. He seemed in strife almost recklessly and desperately to seek death where it was most likely to be found. No Indian ever preceded him in the attack or pursuit of an enemy. No one knew better than he how to ferret out the windings of the Indian's cautious trail. No one could sooner find and seize upon all the secrets of an enemy's camp.*
>
> *He was as cunning as the prairie wolf. He was a perfect woodsman. He could endure any kind of fatigue and privation as well as the best trained Indians. He studied men. There was nothing that an Indian could do, that Rose did not make himself master of. He knew all that Indians knew. He was a great man in his situation.*

During Rose's third year with the Crows he struck a blow for the tribe which changed his name from Cut-Nose to the Five Scalps. He was lounging in his lodge when a squaw raced her pony into camp, screaming that her husband had been killed by Minnetaree warriors and that she had been hit by their arrows.

Instantly Rose and fifty followers took up the trail. After a few miles they spied a column of dust on the opposite side of a ridge, and Rose called to his companions to cross over quickly in order to take the enemy by surprise and count coup (gain the great honor which a warrior receives for striking a living enemy).

The Crows rushed over the ridge and found themselves

in the midst of the Minnetarees. But before they could strike, the quarry escaped onto a prairie. For five miles the Crows pursued their enemies. They could have shot them off their horses, but Rose shouted orders to overtake them and count coup. At the end of the prairie stood a grove of timber which contained many large rocks jutting out from the ground to form a natural fort. The spot was well known to the Minnetarees, and they rode for it with the intention of dismounting and making a stand.

Just as the last enemy entered the wood, Rose rode within reach of his horse's tail. He seized it with his right hand and wheeled his own mount to one side. Down went the enemy's pony, and instantly the Crows were upon him, each leaping to the ground to give the warrior a blow while the spark of life remained in him.

This incident lasted only a few moments, but it gave the Minnetarees time to roll rocks into the openings of the natural fort and to take up strong defensive positions. The Crows greatly outnumbered their enemies, but they knew how dangerous it would be to attack such a well-protected and bravely defended position.

While the Crows held a council, Rose grew more and more enraged at the delay. Finally, he turned on his followers with taunts which he knew would shame them into action.

"You are dogs," he shouted, "that dare not bite until the wolf no longer shows his teeth. You would run from a dead badger on the prairie. Pull open your shirts and let me see if you are not all squaws. Follow me, and if you are afraid, let me hold your shields before you!"

Shouting their battle cry, the Crows leaped forward to storm the enemy stronghold. Undaunted, the Minnetarees fired their few rifles, and five Crow warriors writhed on the ground. Rose rushed up the slope and scaled the rocks at the crest. With one foot on top of the barricade he gave the war whoop. But no **61**

Crow warrior took up the cry. Glancing behind him, he saw his companions fleeing to get out of range. The black chief was more disgusted than alarmed by their desertion. Deliberately turning his back on the Minnetarees, he stalked back down the slope.

The Crows were amazed to see Rose approaching through a hail of bullets and arrows. Surely, they murmured, this black man must have medicine strong enough to overcome death. They gathered around him, but disdainfully he motioned with his foot for them to keep away. "Why don't you cut your own throats and save the Minnetarees the trouble?" he taunted.

Snatching up two thick buffalo-hide shields, he placed them one in front of the other. "Stay like deer where you are," he ordered. Then, armed only with a battle-ax and a knife, he ran forward alone to attack. Knowing that the Minnetarees' rock fort was too small to allow freedom of action, he believed that one determined warrior could leap into their midst and drive them into the open.

Rose reached the top of the wall and hesitated just long enough to raise his battle-ax. That instant two or three rifleshots struck his shield with such force that he fell backward, apparently shot to death. But the black chieftain was far from finished. The victory cry of the Minnetarees died in their throats, for Rose had scrambled up and was in their den. So amazed were the Indians that they seemed unable to defend themselves. Rose fell on them like a wolf in a sheepfold. He split three skulls with his ax. A fourth warrior leaped down on him, only to be impaled on Rose's knife in midair. As the others ran for their lives, Rose pursued long enough to kill a fifth enemy, then stood to one side to watch the Crows complete the work of destruction.

The one-man assault on the Minnetarees was only one of Rose's amazing adventures. In 1811 he made a trip with a French trader to the Snake Indians in Idaho. Before beginning his return journey, he gave all their weapons to some Indians. When the Frenchman complained that they would starve, Rose sharpened a stick, ran down a buffalo, and killed it with a single thrust.

About the same time he was employed as a guide, interpreter, and hunter by Wilson Price Hunt, who was leading a party of traders from St. Louis to the post of Astoria on the Pacific coast. Along the trail Hunt became suspicious that Rose was trying to get his men to desert, telling them that "they would soon become great men among the Crows and have the finest women, and the daughters of chiefs for wives; and the horses and goods they carried off would make them rich for life." Although his suspicions probably were groundless, Hunt paid Rose his full salary to be rid of him halfway through the trip.

In 1812 Rose patched up his dispute with Manuel Lisa. He was visiting Lisa's Missouri River trading post when 200 Cheyenne warriors treatened to destroy it and kill the traders. Lisa tricked the chiefs into holding a council in a room in the fort and stationed Rose at the door to prevent their escape. Then he announced to the other Cheyennes that if they wanted war, Rose would kill their chiefs. In helpless rage the warriors called to the chiefs to fight their way out. Two of them tried, and Rose felled both with his war club. The Cheyennes knew his reputation and made no more trouble at Lisa's trading post.

In 1816 Rose left the West for a while and went to New Orleans. It has been charged that he became an outlaw. Washington Irving wrote that he "belonged to one of the gangs of pirates who infested the islands of the Mississippi, plundering boats as they went down the river, and who sometimes shifted the scenes of their robberies to the shore, waylaying travellers as they returned by land from New Orleans with the proceeds of their downward voyage, plundering them of their money and effects, and often perpetrating the most atrocious murders." **63**

Hiram Chittenden, however, has defended Rose's reputation. Chittenden wrote a history of the American fur trade in which he states that everything definite that is known of Rose is to his credit. "If judgment were to be passed only on the record as it came down to us, he would stand as high as any character in the history of the fur trade."

By 1823 Rose had returned to the West. He joined a large band of trappers employed by William Ashley and set out with them to ascend the Missouri River in two steamboats. The boats arrived at the Arikara villages on May 30, 1823. Rose was an old friend of the Arikaras, so he spent the night in their village. About forty of the trappers slept on shore while Ashley and the others remained on board. In the middle of the night Rose shook Ashley awake and warned him that the Indians planned to attack the trappers at sunrise. Ashley disregarded the warning and left his men on shore. When the Indians attacked, just as Rose had predicted, thirteen trappers were killed, and the others barely escaped by swimming to the boats. While his companions were swimming for their lives, Rose hid himself in a thicket and fired at every Indian in sight. Finally, he plunged into the river and swam for the boats while rifle balls kicked up the water all around him. He was the last man to clamber aboard.

On June 18 the boats reached Fort Atkinson, and Ashley informed Colonel Henry Leavenworth of the attack. Leavenworth ordered out six companies of infantry to punish the Indians. The troops and trappers joined forces to attack the villages, which were protected by high walls of pickets. Among those appointed to the office of ensign was Edward Rose.

The soldiers bombarded the towns until the Indians asked for a parley. Treachery was suspected, and Rose volunteered to enter the village alone. He returned unharmed to report the Indians ready for peace. Colonel Leavenworth wrote in his

64 official report that:

*I had not found any one willing to go into those villages,
except a man by the name of Rose. He appeared to be a brave
and enterprising man, and was well acquainted with those
Indians. He had resided for about three years with them; understood their language, and they were much attached to him. He
was with General Ashley when he was attacked. The Indians
at that time called to him to take care of himself, before they
fired upon General Ashley's party.*

After the Arikara fight, the trappers fanned out into the
mountains. Rose wintered with the Crows on the Wind River.
There he was regarded as the greatest of chiefs. His word was
law.

In the summer of 1824 Rose fell into the hands of the
Blackfeet, a powerful enemy tribe. It was a tradition among
Plains Indians to give a brave enemy a chance to make "the
race for life." The Blackfeet presented this opportunity to the
famous black chief of the Crows. With a 100-step head start,
Rose dashed for some timber. When the Blackfeet headed him
off, he swerved for a river and dived under an enormous log-
jam. The Indians scrambled over the logs, but Rose had disappeared. Finally, they set fire to the wood, shouting that if he
were alive, they would burn him out.

But Rose was concealed between logs in the thickest part
of the raft. He could keep his head above water without being
seen or duck beneath the surface if the smoke threatened to
smother him. Finally, the Indians called that if he would come
out, he could have another chance to run. When he kept silent,
they believed that he had drowned. In great disappointment
they mounted their ponies and rode away.

During the next eight years Rose survived so many adventures that he must have begun to believe that his life was
charmed. But there was one final episode, and then the story

of Edward Rose is told. In 1833 Rose, Hugh Glass, and a man named Menard left Fort Cass for a walk beside the Yellowstone River and fell into an Arikara ambush. Not much is known of Menard, but Glass was a former pirate and a famous mountain man. Once he had crawled 100 miles to overtake two companions who had abandoned him for dead after he had been mauled by a grizzly bear.

There were no witnesses to the massacre of Menard, Glass, and Rose, but one account has it that the Indians surrounded them and set fire to the grass. The trappers saw that they were about to be burned to death, so they blew themselves up with a keg of gunpowder.

The truth of this story cannot be determined, but it would seem to provide a fitting conclusion to the lives of such reckless rascals as Hugh Glass and Ed Rose.

A MISSIONARY TO THE WYANDOTS

John Stewart was born of free parents in Powhatan County, Virginia, in 1786. The family belonged to the Baptist Church, and one of his brothers was a minister of that faith. John's health was poor (he blamed his illness on the wild life he led before he became a Methodist missionary), and he was a victim of consumption during his entire life among the Indians.

During Stewart's youth his parents moved to Tennessee, leaving him in Virginia to learn the dyer's trade. When he became twenty-one, he set out alone for Marietta, Ohio. On his way through the wilderness he fell among robbers and lost all his possessions except the clothes on his back. Upon reaching Marietta, the destitute young black man began to drink heavily, working at his trade only enough to earn money for liquor. His **67** nervous system was wrecked, and his hands trembled so badly that he could scarcely hold a glass to his lips.

Stewart was frightened into changing his life by the sudden death of a drinking companion. Resolving to make another attempt "to seek mercy and pardon at the hands of God," he attended a frontier camp meeting, and the Reverend Marcus Lindsey converted him to Methodism. A strong impression was made on his mind that it was his purpose in life to bring the counsel of God to the heathen of the world. This call was strengthened in 1814, when he became critically ill. He promised that if he recovered, he would become a missionary.

John Stewart did recover, and he felt an inner voice directing him to preach the Gospel to some tribe of Indians located to the northwest. "I, at length, concluded," he wrote, "that if God would enable me to pay my debts, which I had contracted in the days of my wickedness and folly, I would go. This I was enabled to do; and I accordingly took my knapsack, and set off to the Northwest, not knowing whither I was to go. When I set off, my soul was very happy, and I steered my course, sometimes in the road, and sometimes through the woods, till I came to Goshen, on the Tuscarawas River. This was the old Moravian establishment among the Delawares."

Stewart remained several days at Goshen, learning all that he could about the less civilized tribes farther to the north. Then he went on to Pipestown, on the Sandusky River, where a remnant of the once-powerful Delaware nation lived under the leadership of a son of Captain Pipe, the famous war chief who had burned Colonel William Crawford at the stake. While Stewart was at Pipestown, the warriors held a dance, leaping and yelling so fiercely that he feared for his life. When the dancers stopped to rest, Stewart suddenly began singing a hymn in his deep, melodious voice. The unexpected act awed the

Delawares, and they sat in perfect silence. Later they invited him to remain at Pipestown, but he had a strong feeling that he had not yet reached the right place. Leaving the Delawares, he tramped farther into the wilderness, fearing that he might be killed by the first Indian he met.

When he reached Upper Sandusky, Stewart found himself at the recently established Wyandot Reservation. Indian Agent William Walker had charge of this warlike tribe, which as an ally of the British had brought death and destruction throughout Kentucky during the American Revolution. By 1814 the Wyandots had been reduced to about 700 people by war and disease, and those who remained were so much given to drunkenness that scarcely a sober man could be found.

When Stewart presented himself to the agent, he could show no credentials from the Methodist Church. Indeed he had left Marietta without making his intentions known to church officials. Walker suspected that he was a runaway slave and questioned him closely. But Stewart described the circumstances of his conversion with such sincerity that the agent accepted his story. Mrs. Walker, who was half Wyandot, was so greatly impressed by the zeal of the young black man that she became a Methodist convert. As a result of this favorable reception, Stewart was convinced that he had found the place for his mission.

After having satisfied himself of Stewart's good intentions, Agent Walker sent him to see Jonathan Pointer, a Negro who had been captured as a boy by the Wyandots. Pointer and his master had been hoeing corn near Point Pleasant, Virginia, when the Indians rushed from the forest, shot the farmer, and carried the young slave into captivity. Having lived with the Wyandots many years, he spoke their language fluently.

Stewart asked Pointer to assist the mission by translating his sermons. At first, however, Pointer attempted to make excuses. He considered the missionary too religious and hoped **69** he would go away. Pointer confided later that he "wanted a religion that did not fit so close, but gave him leave to indulge in sin."

The day after Stewart's arrival Pointer attended an Indian ceremony and reluctantly permitted the missionary to go with him. At the end of the ceremony Pointer introduced him to the Indians and translated a brief sermon. Stewart followed up with a hymn, then invited the Wyandots to meet with him at Pointer's house next day. Thus, he began a successful campaign to Christianize the Indians, for beginning with a single old squaw, his following grew until he had gained a large number of converts. In time, Pointer became his dedicated assistant.

In February, 1817, Stewart preached about the Last Judgment with startling results. A small number of Indians were praying while a crowd stood nearby to look on and scoff. Suddenly some of the spectators were struck to the ground by an unseen power. Several warriors cried aloud for mercy; others lay stiff and motionless. Those who were not directly affected stared in amazement at the power of the black "medicine man."

In preaching Christianity to the Indians, Stewart made enemies of white whiskey traders and some of the Wyandot chiefs. Once, when he was away from the reservation, the traders spread the word among the Indians that his master had come from Virginia and taken him away in chains. When this rumor was proved false, they urged the Wyandots to chase him away because "Negroes were not acceptable to white people as preachers and it was a disgrace to an Indian nation to continue to listen to him."

Several of the older chiefs defended their native religion in debate with the missionary. When Stewart said that their form of religion was unacceptable to the Lord, Chief John Hicks arose and answered the charge:

My friend, as you have given liberty to any one who had objected to the doctrines you teach to speak on the subject, and state their objections; I, for one, feel myself called upon to rise in defence of the religion of my fathers;—a system of religion the Great Spirit has given his red children, as their guide and rule of their faith, and we are not going to abandon it so soon as you might wish; we are contented with it, because it suits our conditions and is adapted to our capacities. Cast your eyes abroad over the world, and see how many different systems of religion there are in it—there are almost as many different systems as there are nations—say this is not the work of the Lord.

When John Hicks stopped speaking, Chief Monocue arose and objected to Stewart's attempt to lead them to accept the Bible as their guide:

I do not doubt that you state faithfully what your book says; but let me correct an error into which you appear to have run, and that is your belief that the Great Spirit designed that his red children should be instructed out of it. This is a mistake, the Great Spirit never designed this to be the case; he never intended that they should be instructed out of a book, a thing which properly belongs to those who made it and can understand what it says; it is a plant that cannot grow and flourish among red people. Ours is a religion that suits us red people, and we intend to keep it and preserve it sacred among us, believing that the Great Spirit gave it to our grandfathers in ancient days.

The most dangerous of Stewart's Indian enemies was Chief Two-Logs (also called Bloody Eyes). This violent man did his best to discredit the missionary, claiming that Indians were created by the Great Spirit but Negroes by the Evil Spirit. On one occasion Stewart attended a house-raising, and Two- **71**

Logs suddenly began arguing with him because he had preached against Indian dancing and feasting:

I do not believe the Great Spirit will punish his red children for dancing and feasting. Yet I cannot say that he will not punish white people for doing these things; for to me it looks quite probable the Great Spirit has forbidden these things among the whites, because they are naturally wicked, quarrelsome and contentious; for it is a truth they cannot deny, that they cannot have a dance, a feast, or any public amusement, but some will get drunk, quarrel, fight, or do something wrong.

Two-Logs glared at Stewart so fiercely while he spoke that the missionary expected his life to be threatened. But then the chief turned on his own younger brother, Between-the-Logs, who was a follower of Stewart's, and beat him severely, threatening to kill him if he did not renounce Christianity within one year.

Between-the-Logs was a firm convert, and no threat could make him give up the Christian religion. Years after the beating he told the history of Wyandot religion and included a tribute to the teachings of John Stewart:

Will you have patience to hear me, and I will give you a history of religion among the Indians for some time back, and how we have been deceived. Our fathers had a religion of their own, by which they served God, and were happy before any white man came among them. They used to worship with feasts, sacrifices, dances, and rattles; in doing which they thought they were right. Our parents wished us to be good, and they used to make us do good, and would sometimes correct us for doing evil. But a great while ago the French sent us the good Book by a Roman priest, and we listened to him. He taught us that we must confess our sins, and he would forgive them; that we must worship Lady Mary, and do penance. He

Between-the-Logs, Wyandot chief and one of John Stewart's converts to Christianity. Between-the-Logs defended Stewart in spite of threats on his life by Chief Bloody Eyes.   (*Smithsonian Institution*)

told us to pray, and to carry the cross on our breasts. He told us also that it was wrong to drink whisky. But we found that he would drink it himself, and we followed his steps and got drunk too. At last our priest left us, and this religion all died away. Then we thought we would return to our fathers' religion again. So many of us left off getting drunk, and we began again to do pretty well. Then the Seneca prophet arose, and pretended that he had talked to the Great Spirit, and that he had told him what Indians ought to do. So we heard and followed him. It is true, he told us many good things, and that we ought not to drink whisky; but soon we found that he would tell us we must not do things, and yet do them himself. So we were deceived again.

After some time the great Shawnee prophet arose. Well, we heard him, and some of us followed him for a while. But we watched him very closely, and soon found him like all the rest. Then we left him also; and now we were made strong in **73** *the religion of our fathers, and concluded to turn away from it no more, when the war broke out between our father, the President, and King George. Our nation was for war with the King, and every man wanted to be a big man. Then we drank whisky, and fought; and, by the time the war was over, we were all scattered, and many killed and dead. But the chiefs thought they would gather the nation together once more. We had a good many collected, and were again establishing our Indian religion. Just at this time a black man, our brother here, came to us and told us he was sent by the Great Spirit to tell us the true and good way. But we thought he was like all the rest; that he wanted to cheat us, and get our money and land from us. He told us all our sins; showed us that drinking whisky was ruining us; that the Great Spirit was angry with us; and that we must leave off these things. But we treated him ill, and gave him but little to eat, and trampled on him, and were jealous of him for a year. We are sure, if the Great Spirit had not sent him, he could not have borne with our treatment.*

About this time he talked about leaving us, to see his friends; and our squaws told us that we were fools to let him go, for the great God had sent him, and we ought to adopt him. But still we wanted to hear longer. They then told us what God had done for them by this man. So we attended his meeting in the council-house, and the Great Spirit came upon us so that some cried aloud, some clapped their hands, some ran away, and some were angry. We held our meeting all night, sometimes singing and sometimes praying. By this time we were convinced that God had sent him to us; and then we adopted him, and gave him mother and children. Now some of us are trying to do good, and are happy.

In 1818 some missionaries of another church visited Sandusky on their way northward and offered Stewart a good salary if he would go with them. When he refused, they asked to see his Methodist credentials, and he told them quite frankly that he was there without the church's knowledge. As a result of this episode, Stewart got in touch with Methodist authorities for the first time and they were amazed to learn that he was among the Indians and that his mission was succeeding. In 1820 Stewart married a woman of his race, and as a result of the efforts of church leaders, he was given a home and a 60-acre farm at the edge of the reservation. His illness had become serious by that time, and other preachers were sent to take charge of the mission. He continued his labors, however, until the fall of 1823, when he became unable to leave his bed. He died of consumption on December 17 of that year.

In judging the success of John Stewart's mission, it is helpful to compare the condition of the Wyandots at the time he came to them with their situation near the end of his labors. Shortly before his death he wrote to a friend concerning this matter:

> *The situation of the Wyandot nation when I first arrived among them, near six years ago, may be judged from their manner of living. Some of their houses were made of small poles, others of bark. The women did nearly all the work. In a word, they were really in a savage state. But now they are building hewed log-houses, cultivating their lands, and successfully adopting the various agricultural arts. They now manifest a relish for civilization; and it is probable that some of them will, this year, raise an ample support for their families from the produce of their farms. There are more than two hundred of them who have renounced heathenism, and embraced Christianity.*

He might have added that among his converts were Chiefs John Hicks and Monacue. And although Stewart didn't know it, even brutal old Bloody Eyes would accept Christianity before he died.

JIM BECKWOURTH, THE MOUNTAIN MAN

James Pierson Beckwith (usually known as Jim Beckwourth) was born on April 26, 1798, at Fredericksburg, Virginia. His father was a planter and a major in the American Revolution. His mother was a Negro slave. In 1810 Major Beckwith moved to Missouri and bought a large tract of land near St. Louis.

In his youth Jim probably was his father's slave. He was assigned to learn the blacksmith trade, but he seized the first opportunity to escape to the West. In the fall of 1823 he signed up with General William Ashley's fur company, joining such famous mountain men as Jim Bridger, Hugh Glass, Cut-Nose Rose, the Sublette brothers, and many others.

Jim was employed as a blacksmith but soon proved worthy

of more important assignments. During 1824 he purchased horses from the Pawnee Indians for Ashley's trappers to use in exploring the Rocky Mountains. In 1825 he learned to trap beaver, and a year later he went with William Sublette, Jim Bridger, and others into the Yellowstone country. There they encountered the Blackfeet, the fiercest and largest tribe in that region. The trappers were suspicious when some Blackfoot chiefs invited the party to establish a trading post among them. Sublette called for volunteers, and the only men willing to risk their scalps were Beckwourth and his young friend Baptiste. The pair obtained thirty-nine packs of beaver in three weeks from the Blackfeet.

Jim's success with the tribe was not limited to fur trading. He claimed that he married the chief's daughter. When he caught her dancing around the scalps of white men, he struck her so hard that he believed he had killed her. The enraged Blackfeet were ready to burn him alive, but the chief came to his rescue, ruling that since the girl was married to Beckwourth, he had every right to kill her. To prove he meant what he said, he presented Jim with his second daughter to wed. To Jim's surprise his first bride recovered and returned to him. Thereafter, both sisters shared his lodge.

This adventure sounds like a tall tale, and Jim Beckwourth's life story, which was written in 1856, has been called one of the greatest collections of lies ever printed. On the other hand, many historians have relied on it in writing books about the fur trade in the Rocky Mountains. Most mountain men were known to stretch the truth when describing their own exploits, and Jim was one of the best of them.

The following adventure, selected from his life story, is no tall tale. It was shared by fur company officials who published a similar account of many of the incidents which Beckwourth described.

On our way to the rendezvous we heard singing in our rear, and, looking in the direction of the noise, we discovered a party of five hundred mounted Indians coming directly toward us. "Flat Heads! Flat Heads!" was shouted; and, believing them to be such, I and my two friends wheeled to go and meet them. Approaching within a short distance, to our horror and surprise we discovered they were Black Feet—a tribe who prize white scalps very highly. Wishing to take us all together, probably, they ordered us back—an order we obeyed with alacrity, and we speedily gave the alarm. Placing the women and children in advance, and directing them to make all speed to a patch of willows six miles in front, and there to secure themselves, we formed to hold the Indians in check. The women made good time, considering the jaded state of their animals, for they were all accustomed to horseback-riding.

By this time the Indians had commenced charging upon us, not so furiously as was their wont, but they doubtless considered their prey sure, and, farther, did not care to come into too close proximity to our rifles. Situated as we were, it was impossible for them to surround us, for we had a lake on one side and a mountain on the other. They knew, however, that we must emerge into the open country, where their chance of attack would be improved. When they approached too near, we used our rifles, and always with effect; our women the mean while urging on their animals with all the solicitude of mothers, who knew that capture was certain death to their offspring.

The firing continued between both parties during the whole time of our retreat to the willows; in fact, it was a running fight through the whole six miles. On the way we lost one man, who was quite old. He might have saved himself by riding to the front, and I repeatedly urged him to do so, telling him that he could not assist us; but he refused even to spur on his horse when the Indians made their charges. I tarried with him, urging him on, until I found it would be certain death to delay longer. My horse had scarcely made three leaps in advance

when I heard him cry, "Oh God, I am wounded!" Wheeling

my horse, I called on my companions to save him. I returned to him, and found an arrow trembling in his back. I jerked it out, and gave his horse several blows to quicken his pace; but the poor old man reeled and fell from his steed, and the Indians were upon him in a moment to tear off his scalp. This delay nearly cost two more lives, for myself and Jarvey were surrounded with the Black Feet, and their triumphant yells told us they felt certain of their prey. Our only chance of escape was to leap a slough fifteen feet from bank to bank, which we vaulted over at full speed. One Indian followed us, but he was shot in the back directly upon reaching the bank, and back he rolled into the ditch. We passed on around the slough in order to join our companions, but in doing so were compelled to charge directly through a solid rank of Indians. We passed with the rapidity of pigeons, escaping without any damage to ourselves or horses, although a shower of arrows and bullets whistled all around us. As we progressed, their charges became more frequent and daring; our ammunition now grew very short, and we never used a charge without we were sure of its paying for itself.

At length we gained the willows. If our ammunition had been plenty, we would have fought them here as long as they might have wished. When all was gone, what were we to do with an enemy more than ten times our number, who never grants or receives quarter?

Eroquey proposed one bold charge for the sake of the women and children. "Let us put our trust in God," he exclaimed, "and if we are to die, let us fall in protecting the defenseless. They will honor our memory for the bravery they witnessed."

Sixteen of us accordingly mounted our horses, leaving the remainder to hold out to the last. Eroquey led the charge. In our fierce onset we broke through two ranks of mounted Indians, killing and overturning every thing in our way. Unfortunately, my beautiful horse was killed in his tracks, leaving me alone amid a throng of Indians. I was wounded with an arrow in the **79** head, the scar of which, with many other wounds received since, I shall carry to my grave. My boy Baptiste, seeing my danger, called upon his comrades to assist him to save his brother. They charged a second time, and the Indians who surrounded me were driven back. At that moment Baptiste rode up to me; I sprang on the saddle behind him, and retreated in safety to the willows. The foe still pressed us sorely, but their shots produced little effect except to cut off the twigs of the bushes which formed our hiding-place; as for charging in upon us, they showed some disinclination.

To hold out much longer was impossible. Immediately assistance must be had, and it could come from no other place than our camp. To risk a message there seemed to subject the messenger to inevitable death; yet the risk must be encountered by some one. "Who'll go? who'll go?" was asked on all sides. I was wounded, but not severely; and, at a time so pressing, I hardly knew that I was wounded at all. I said, "Give me a swift horse, and I will try to force my way. Do not think I am anxious to leave you in your perilous position."

"You will run the greatest risk," said they. "But if you go, take the best horse."

Campbell then said that two had better go, for there might be a chance of one living to reach the camp. Calhoun volunteered to accompany me, if he had his choice of horses, to which no one raised any objection. Disrobing ourselves, then, to the Indian costume, and tying a handkerchief round our heads, we mounted horses as fleet as the wind, and bade the little band adieu. "God bless you!" shouted the men; the women cried, "The Great Spirit preserve you, my friends."

Again we dashed through the ranks of the foe before they had time to comprehend our movement. The balls and arrows flew around us like hail, but we escaped uninjured. Some of the Indians darted in pursuit of us, but, seeing they could not overtake us, returned to their ranks. Our noble steeds seemed to fully understand the importance of the mission they were going on. When about five miles from the camp we saw a party *of our men approaching us at a slow gallop. We halted instantly, and, taking our saddle-blankets, signaled to them first for haste, and then that there was a fight. Perceiving this, one man wheeled and returned to the camp, while the others quickened their pace, and were with us in a moment, although they were a mile distant when we made the signal. There were only sixteen, but on they rushed, eager for the fray, and still more eager to save our friends from a horrible massacre. They all turned out from the camp, and soon the road was lined with men, all hurrying along at the utmost speed of the animals they bestrode. My companion and I returned with the first party, and, breaking once more through the enemy's line, rode back into the willows, amid the cheers of our companions and the loud acclamations of the women and children, who now breathed more freely again. The Indians were surprised at seeing a re-enforcement, and their astonishment was increased when they saw a whole line of men coming to our assistance. They instantly gave up the battle and commenced a retreat. We followed them about two miles, until we came to the body of Bolliere—the old man that had been slain; we then returned, bringing his mangled remains with us.*

On our side we lost four men killed and seven wounded. Not a woman or child was injured. From the enemy we took seventeen scalps, most of them near the willows; those that we killed on the road we could not stop for. We were satisfied they had more than a hundred slain; but as they always carry off their dead, we could not ascertain the exact number. We also lost two packs of beavers, a few packs of meat, together with some valuable horses.

After attending to our wounded, we all proceeded to camp, where the scalp-dance was performed by all the half-breeds and women, many of the mountaineers taking part in the dance. The battle lasted five hours, and never in my whole life had I run such danger of losing my life and scalp. I now began to deem myself Indian-proof, and to think I never should be killed by them.

81

In September, 1828, Beckwourth and Caleb Greenwood, a trapper married to a Crow woman, visited his squaw's village. Greenwood told the Crows that Beckwourth was an Indian who had been captured as a small boy and raised by the whites. An old Crow woman decided that Jim was her long-lost son, and the tribe invited him to become one of them. Here was a fine opportunity to get valuable furs, so Jim decided to accept their invitation. He adopted the life of an Indian, fought in their battles against enemy tribes, and proved himself to be such a brave warrior that he gained great influence over the Crows. Eventually he was chosen their chief and married ten of the prettiest girls in the nation.

Jim lived with the Crows for at least six years. Then he returned to St. Louis, where he signed up as a scout in the war against the Florida Seminole Indians. As ready to fight in swamps as mountains, he shot it out with the Seminoles in the bloody Battle of Okeechobee.

Returning to the West, he established trading posts in New Mexico and Colorado. In 1844 he went to California and served as a dispatch rider in the Mexican War. During the gold rush he discovered a pass through the Sierra Nevada, which is still known as Beckwourth Pass, and settled there for a while, operating a trading post and hotel.

Beckwourth's autobiography ended in California but he was still to experience many thrilling adventures. His later career was skillfully sketched by Nolie Mumey in a book entitled *James Pierson Beckwourth, 1856–1866*.

James P. Beckwourth, one of the most famous of the mountain men. Beckwourth, whose mother was a slave, became an Indian chief and fought in some of the fiercest battles in frontier history.
(*Library, State Historical Society of Colorado*)

In 1852 Jim moved to Westport, Missouri, and later he established a ranch near Denver. In 1862, despite the fact that he was sixty-four years old, he tried to volunteer to serve his country in the Civil War. He was turned down, but two years later the Army found that it could still make good use of his scouting abilities. Colonel J. M. Chivington of the Colorado Volunteers recruited him to guide an expedition against the Cheyenne Indians. Jim led the force of 750 men on a five-day march across the snow-covered plains. The night of November 28 was so bitterly cold that the old frontiersman became almost too stiff to follow the trail, but he brought the soldiers to the Cheyenne village on Sand Creek just before dawn.

Chivington showed no mercy to the sleeping Indians. At daybreak he sent the troops thundering down on the village, and when a chief rushed forward making signs of peace, the white men opened fire. Then, with Chivington shouting, "Kill and scalp all Indians, nits make lice," they massacred men, women, and children. Chivington reported 600 Indians killed, and most of them were scalped.

Jim deeply regretted his part in the massacre. In January, 1865, he located the remnants of the shattered Cheyenne nation about 100 miles from Denver, and although the Indians knew that he had been at Sand Creek, he rode boldly into their camp and urged them to make peace. When the United States government held an investigation of the Sand Creek massacre, Jim told of his meeting with the tribe:

I told them that I had come to persuade them to make peace with the whites, as there were not enough of them left to fight the whites. "We know it," was the general response of the council. "But what do we want to live for? The white man has taken our country, killed all our game; was not satisfied with that but killed our wives and children. Now no peace. We want to go and meet our families in the spirit land. We loved the whites until we found out they lied to us, and robbed us of what we had. We have raised the battle-axe until death."

They asked me then why I had come to Sand Creek with the soldiers to show them the country. I told them if I had not come the white chief would have hung me.

After the Sand Creek affair Jim gave up ranching. He trapped on the Green River until the Blackfeet killed three of his men and stole all his horses. Then, in 1866, he was hired by Colonel Henry B. Carrington to accompany the cavalry to Montana. The Crow Indians were becoming hostile, and the soldiers wanted the former chief, Beckwourth, to serve as peace-maker. Accompanied by only one trooper, Jim rode into the Crow village. A few days later the soldier brought word that the old Negro frontiersman had died in the lodge of the chief.

There is a legend that Jim was poisoned when he refused the invitation of the Crows to resume his life with them. The Indians believed that if they could not keep him as a living chief, they would at least preserve his strong medicine in the tribal burying ground.

A GIANT WITH LEWIS AND CLARK

Just as Estevanico trudged beside his Spanish master from the Gulf Coast to the Pacific Ocean in 1536, almost 300 years later a black man named York struggled over mountains and rivers with the first party to reach the Pacific by the northern overland route. The slave of Captain William Clark, he accompanied his master on one of the most important and dangerous explorations ever attempted. When President Thomas Jefferson called on Captain Clark and Meriwether Lewis to lead a small band of soldiers and frontiersmen across the huge territory recently purchased from France, York was taken along to serve his master. As soon as they were in Indian country, the slave proved to be of great service to the entire expedition and to his country as well.

The Lewis and Clark Expedition left St. Louis in the spring of 1804. After wintering at the Mandan Indian villages far up the Missouri River, the explorers crossed the Rockies on horseback, boated down the Columbia River, and reached the Pacific in November, 1805. After spending a miserable winter near the mouth of the Columbia, the party returned across the mountains and plains and reached St. Louis on September 23, 1806. In constant danger from Indians, bears, snakes, storms, and many other hazards, York and his companions explored the Northwest without losing a man except one who died as a result of illness.

It was no surprise that York proved valuable to the expedition as a hunter, providing the party with every kind of game from squirrel to buffalo. It was known, also, that he spoke some French and could serve in a pinch as interpreter. Unexpected, however, was the giant black man's help in gaining the friendship of the Indians. No Negro had ever been seen by the redskins in that region, and York created a sensation wherever he went. He took pride in demonstrating his great strength and dancing ability. With the expedition was a musician, named Peter Cruzat, who fiddled fast tunes while York performed in a circle of admiring Indians. "I ordered my black Servant to Dance which amused the Croud Verry much and Somewhat astonished them, that so large a man should be active," wrote William Clark in his journal.

On March 9, 1805, the fierce Minnetaree chief called the Borgne visited the expedition. He said that "some foolish young men of his nation had informed him that there was a black man in the party and wished to know if it was true." At that moment York stepped out from behind a tree. The Borgne examined him in amazement; then, according to Clark, "he spit on his hand and rubbed in order to rub off the paint. The Negro pulled off the handkerchief from his head and showed **87** his hair—on which the Borgne was convinced that he was of a different species."

When the expedition approached the Rocky Mountains, the captains tried to persuade some Shoshoni Indians to guide them across before the snow blocked the passes. The Shoshonis were too much afraid of their Blackfoot Indian enemies to come down from their mountain hiding places until they heard that a strange and marvelous black man was in an approaching canoe. Then curiosity overcame fear. The Indians came down to the water's edge, and Lewis and Clark gained information of great importance to the survival of the expedition.

York, when seen from afar by the Flathead Chief Three Eagles, was believed to be painted black for war. But he proved his peaceful intentions by permitting the Indians to try to wash off his "paint" with wet fingers. He pleased and astonished the Flatheads even more with a demonstration of great physical power and dancing ability.

Among the Nez Percés, York's patience finally wore thin when he saw still more Indians spitting on their hands in preparation for the usual attempt to rub off the black paint. He whipped out his knife and glared fiercely, while the Indians hurriedly backed away.

It was the custom among Western Indians to honor important guests by offering food, lodging, and "temporary wives." To refuse was an insult. Both the Mandan and Nez Percé tribes considered York to be a very distinguished visitor and provided him with "appropriate accommodations." On his return trip the following year he learned that he was the father of a number of children. The Indians prized these children, for through them they were able to keep some of the great medicine of this marvelous stranger.

When the Lewis and Clark Expedition disbanded in 1806, **88** York returned to the Clark family home at Louisville. A few years later Clark gave him his freedom. Then he became a freighter, driving a team between Richmond and Nashville. Finally, his business failed, and Clark believed that he died of cholera in Tennessee some time before 1832.

But after that date there took place in the Rocky Mountains a thrilling adventure which may indicate that York still was very much alive. Zenas Leonard was traveling through the Crow Indian country with a band of trappers in the fall of 1832, when he:

found a Negro man who informed us that he first came to this country with Lewis and Clark—with whom he also returned to the State of Missouri, and in a few years returned again with a Mr. Mackinney, a trader on the Missouri River, and has remained here ever since—which is about ten or twelve years. He has acquired a correct knowledge of their manner of living, and speaks their language fluently. He has rose to be a considerable character, or chief, at least he assumes all the dignities of a chief, for he has four wives with whom he lives alternately.

After obtaining the black man's help in recovering some stolen stock, the trappers moved farther into the mountains. In November, 1834, Leonard and his companions returned to the Crow village and visited with the man who claimed to be York. Riding with the Crows on a buffalo hunt, they caught sight of a band of Blackfeet. These enemies barricaded themselves to fight for their lives, and the Crows sent a messenger to their village to bring up every warrior, woman, and child.

Leonard then witnessed one of the most desperate battles in the history of Indian warfare. Not long afterward he published an account of it in which the Negro chief is described as the hero:

This was quite a different kind of sport from that which I expected to witness when I left the Indian camp, but one of **89** *no less interest, and far more important to me. Whilst the express was absent both parties employed their time in strengthening their positions—the Blackfeet had chosen a most fortunate spot to defend themselves, and by a little labour found themselves in a fort that might have done credit to an army of frontier regulars. It was situated on the brow of a hill, in a circle of rocks shaped similar to a horse-shoe, with a ledge of rocks from three to four feet high on either side, and about ten feet, on the part reaching to the brink of the hill, with a very creditable piece of breast work built in front, composed of logs, brush and stones. From their present situation they have a decided advantage over the Crows, and if well prepared for war, could hold out a considerable length of time, and deal destruction thick and fast on any force that might attempt to scale their fort—which looks more like the production of art than nature. Whilst the Blackfeet were assiduously engaged in*

Blackfoot Indians, one of the most warlike tribes of the West. In 1834, a black man who identified himself as York, a member of the Lewis and Clark Expedition, made a one-man assault on a Blackfoot fortress after his Crow Indian companions had been repulsed by the well-armed defenders.

(Library, State Historical Society of Colorado)

defending their position, the Crows were no less idle in pre-
paring for the attack, the destruction of which, they were
determined should not be relaxed as long as there was a living
Blackfoot Indian to be found in the neighborhood. Previous to
the arrival of the reinforcement, which was about ten o'clock,
there had been three Crows and one Blackfoot killed, which
was done at the first attack after the latter were driven into their
fort.

When the express reached the Crow village every man,
woman, and child able to point a gun or mount a horse repaired
with all speed to the scene of action, who came up uttering the
most wild and piercing yells I ever heard in my life. A great
deal of contention at first took place among the principal men
of the Crow tribe as to the manner of attacking their enemy,
who appeared to look down upon them in defiance; not with-
standing the Crows kept up a continual yelling and firing of
guns, all of which was without effect. Finally they appeared to
harmonize and understand each other.

As matters now seemed to indicate the approach of a crisis,
I repaired to an eminence about 200 yards from the fort among
some cedar trees, where I had an excellent view of all their
movements. At first the Crows would approach the fort by two
or three hundred in a breast, but on arriving near enough to do
any execution, the fire from the fort would compel them to
retreat. They then formed in a trail along the top of the ridge,
and in rotation would ride at full speed past the breast-work,
firing as they passed, and then throwing themselves on the side
of the horse until nothing will be exposed to the enemy except
one arm and one leg. This they found to be very destructive to
their horses and also their men, there being now ten Crows and
several horses laying dead on the field. Urged by their ill suc-
cess thus far, and by the piteous lamentations of the wives,
children and relatives of those who had fell, the Crow Chiefs
decided on suspending the attack, and determined to hold a
council of war for the purpose of deciding on what measures
should be adopted, in order to destroy these brave Blackfeet. **91**

The chiefs held a hasty and stormy council. Some were in favour of abandoning the Blackfeet entirely, & others were determined on charging into their fort and end the battle in a total and bloody massacre. This was finally decided upon, but not until after several speeches were made for and against it, and the pipe of war smoked by each brave and chief.

As soon as this determination of the chiefs was made known the war-whoop again resounded with the most deafening roar through the plain—every voice that was able to make a noise was strained to its very utmost to increase the sound, until the very earth, trees and rocks seemed to be possessed of vocal powers. By their tremendous howling they had worked as great a change in the courage of their soldiery, as the most soul-enlivening martial music would the cowardly fears of a half-intoxicated militia company.

Now was the moment for action. Each man appeared willing to sacrifice his life if it would bring down an enemy; and in this spirit did they renew and repeat the attack on the breast-work of their enemy, but as often did they retreat with severe loss. Again and again did they return to the charge, but all was of no use—all their efforts were of no avail—confusion began to spread through their ranks—many appeared over-whelmed with despair—and the whole Crow nation was about to retreat from the field, when the negro, who has been hereto-fore mentioned, and who had been in company with us, ad-vanced a few steps towards the Crows and ascended a rock from which he addressed the Crow warriors in the most earnest and impressive manner. He told them that they had been here making a great noise, as if they could kill the enemy by it—that they had talked long and loud about going into the fort, and that the white men would say the Indian had a crooked tongue, when talking about his war exploits. He told them that their hearts were small, and that they were cowardly—that they acted more like squaws than men, and were not fit to defend their hunting ground. He told them that the white men were
92 *ashamed of them and would refuse to trade with such a nation*

of cowards—that the Blackfeet would go home and tell their people that three thousand Crows could not take a handful of them,—that they would be laughed at, scorned, and treated with contempt by all nations wherever known—that no tribe would degrade themselves hereafter by waging war with them, and that the whole Crow nation, once so powerful, would forever after be treated as a nation of squaws. The old negro continued in this strain until they became greatly animated, & told them that if the red man was afraid to go amongst his enemy, he would show them that a black man was not, and he leaped from the rock on which he had been standing, and, looking neither to the right nor to the left, made for the fort as fast as he could run. The Indians guessing his purpose, and inspired by his words and fearless example, followed close to his heels, and were in the fort dealing destruction to the right and left nearly as soon as the old man.

Here now was a scene of no common occurrence. A space of ground about the size of an acre, completely crowded with hostile Indians fighting for life, with guns, bows and arrows, knives and clubs, yelling and screaming until the hair seemed to lift the caps from our heads. As soon as most of the Crows got into the fort, the Blackfeet began to make their escape out of the opposite side, over the rocks about 10 feet high. Here they found themselves no better off, as they were immediately surrounded and hemmed in on all sides by overwhelming numbers. A large number on both sides had fell in the engagement in the inside of the fort, as there the Crows had an equal chance with their enemy, but when on the outside the advantage was decidedly against them, as they were confined in a circle and cut down in a few moments. When the Blackfeet found there was no chance of escape, they fought with more than human desperation. From the time they left their fort, they kept themselves in regular order, moving forward in a solid breast, cutting their way through with their knives, until their last man fell, pierced, perhaps, with a hundred wounds.

Leonard's account of this battle, published in a Pennsylvania newspaper, probably never was seen on the frontier. But the black man's exploit was told and retold by trappers, sitting around Rocky Mountain campfires, as long as the fur trade lasted. Most of them believed that the hero was Jim Beckwourth, rather than York. Beckwourth was glad to take the credit, and he even included an account of the battle in his autobiography. But Beckwourth was a young man in 1834 and does not fit the "old Negro" described by Leonard. Historians believe that the black man was neither York nor Beckwourth, but Cut-Nose Rose. But this could hardly be true if Rose had been killed in an Arikara ambush in 1833, as reported by reliable authorities.

If not Beckwourth or Rose, could the Negro who said he was a companion of Lewis and Clark truly have been York? Not if William Clark's belief was correct that he died of cholera before 1832. But John Bakeless, in a book about Lewis and Clark, is not fully convinced. "It is just possible," he wrote, "that York enjoyed freedom more than his old master thought and had preferred to disappear. Was it not better to be a chief with four wives, a victorious warrior among the Crows, than a slave in Kentucky or a struggling freedman in Tennessee?"

York would not have been the first man to find the wild, free life of the Indians desirable once he had experienced it along the trail with Lewis and Clark.

LUIS PACHECO—TRAITOR, SCAPEGOAT, OR PATRIOT?

One of the most extraordinary slaves who ever lived was Luis Pacheco (also known as Louis Fatio). Most of what is known of his early life is due to the research of the historian Kenneth W. Porter, who published accounts of his adventures in the *Journal of Negro History*. Luis was born on December 26, 1800, at the New Switzerland plantation, near Jacksonville, Florida. His African-born parents were slaves of the Fatio family. At a time when the education of slaves was forbidden by law, he was taught to read and write by Susan Philippa Fatio, the young daughter of his master. He easily learned to read English, Spanish, and French. In addition, he learned to speak the Seminole language from an older brother who had been captured as a baby and reared by the Indians.

During his youth the Seminoles visited the plantation frequently, and their unfettered way of life seemed much more enjoyable to Luis than that of a plantation slave. Several times he ran away to stay for short periods with a sister who lived among the Seminoles.

When Luis reached young manhood, he married a slave girl who worked at a St. Augustine plantation. Having run away to see her, he stayed so long that he feared to return to his master. Listed as a runaway, he was finally located at Tampa. There the commanding officer of Fort Brooke bought him to use as post interpreter. Each time the command of the fort changed hands Luis served a new master. Finally, in 1830, Major James McIntosh sold him to Antonio Pacheco, a wealthy Spanish plantation owner. He worked at Pacheco's trading post at Sarasota, and when his master died, he became the property of the widow.

In 1835 the Second Seminole War broke out, largely because the United States government was attempting to move the Indians from their Florida homes to the Indian Territory. Negroes living among the Indians feared that they would be enslaved by the whites. Some of them who held great influence in tribal affairs urged the Seminoles to resist. An incident which led to hostilities was the seizure by white slave hunters of Chief Osceola's Negro wife, Morning Dew. The great Seminole patriot was imprisoned in irons for six days when he protested. To get revenge, he swore to lead his warriors against the entire United States Army if necessary.

On December 17, 1835, the Seminoles attacked several plantations. Osceola ambushed an Army baggage train and fought it out with a relief force of infantry. General Duncan L. Clinch called for reinforcements, and Major Francis L. Dade's infantry company was moved from Key West to Tampa to combine forces with Captain G. W. Gardiner's artillery and

Captain U. S. Frazier's infantry companies. This small army was ordered to move out through the swamps to Fort King.

Since none of the soldiers knew the trail, a dependable guide was needed, not only to pilot the troops through the swamps, but to avoid ambushes as well. Because of his excellent record as interpreter at the post and his knowledge of the Indian country, Luis was leased from Mrs. Pacheco by Captain John C. Casey for $25 per month.

Luis was eager to guide the troops, and he led them into a trap. On the morning of December 28, Major Dade's force of 110 was almost wiped out by some 400 Indians and Negroes who lay in ambush near the Great Wahoo Swamp. Only 3 soldiers escaped from the field, and all of them died of their wounds. At first it was believed that Luis had been killed with the troops. Later, when the soldiers learned that he had joined the Seminoles, they accused him of being a traitor and spy.

General Thomas S. Jesup charged that the guide had "kept up a correspondence with the Seminole Negroes, informing them of the intended march of Major Dade." John Lee Williams, a Florida settler, wrote that Luis "was frequently absent from the troops in the march; he fell on hearing the first gun, but directly after joined the enemy, and read to them the dispatches and papers found upon the dead."

Ohio Congressman Joshua R. Giddings, a strong opponent of slavery, agreed that Luis had conspired with the Seminoles, but instead of condemning him as a traitor, he praised the slave as a patriot:

Luis Pacheco understood the efforts that were being made to enslave his brethren. In revenge for the oppression to which he was subjected, he conceived the purpose of sacrificing a regiment of white men, who were engaged in the support of slavery. Soon as the first fire showed him the precise position **97**

*of his friends, he joined them, and swearing eternal hostility
to all who enslave their fellow men, lent his own efforts in
carrying forward the work of death, until the last individual
of that doomed regiment sunk beneath their tomahawks.*

It is evident that almost everyone believed Luis guilty of
deliberately leading Dade and his troops to their deaths. But
there is another side to this story, and it did not come to light
for fifty-seven years. Incredibly, in 1892, Luis Pacheco appeared
at his old home at New Switzerland and presented himself to
the elderly lady who had taught him to read and write when
both of them were children. Eager to set the record straight
about his part in the Dade massacre, he told his story to a
newspaper reporter. It was published in the October, 1892,
issue of the *Florida Times-Union,* and it provides a vivid account of the battle by the last surviving eyewitness:

*There was a note telling him that Major Belton, in com-
mand of Ft. Clinch, needed him immediately at headquarters.
He proceeded there and Major Belton said that he needed him
as a guide for Major Dade, who had started out the day before
for Ft. King. He obtained the consent of Mrs. Pacheco and
Louis, of course, was willing. He was told that Major Dade
would be found that night camped on the Little Hillsboro'
River. He made hasty preparations to overtake him and naturally made inquiries as to what mission Major Dade and his
hundred odd men were bent on. There were rumors of Indian
depredations, but the rumors were vague and not credited, as
peace between them and the whites had reigned unbroken for
a long period.*

*Louis found, therefore, that the people of Ft. Clinch were
almost unanimously of the impression that the red men were
not hostile. He hurried on the road and late that evening came
upon the troops of Major Dade camped on the Little Hillsboro'.*

The next morning after breakfast he was sent through the woods and swamps to the Big Hillsboro'.

There his suspicions were aroused. In fact, he became frightened. He found the bridge over the river burned and a cow in the road split wide open. He did not know what it meant, but he knew it was a sign of evil omen. He came back and reported the fact to Major Dade.

Major Dade laughed when Louis asked him if the Seminoles were not hostile.

"Hostile? No," said the major. "That's old Bowlegs did that, Louis. He's been in the guard-house at Tampa. He got away a few days ago, and he did that out of spite."

Louis, however, knew more of the Seminoles than Major Dade did, and his fears were not decreased by this light treatment of a serious matter; but it was in vain that he protested that 'more than old Bowlegs did that.'

Nevertheless the troops pushed on and forded the river. On the line of march many houses of settlers were found empty, and even the cattle had been driven away. This heightened the fears of the guide, who felt more than ever that something was wrong, and when told by a colored man on the road that Major Dade had been told that the Indians were going to attack the whites on the Oulthalacoochee (Withalacoochee) river his fears were heightened, as the road to Ft. King led directly across that stream.

Today Louis says: "I believe that Major Dade knew that the Indians were hostile, for I was sent on to explore every bad place."

"If you are afraid, Louis, I will not send you," said the commander.

"Oh, no, major, I'm not afraid. Did not you tell me that the Indians were not hostile?"

"Well, Louis, if they catch you go with them. I'll get you some day."

On the night following the day of the fording of the Big Hillsboro' the command slept at Hagerman's Hole, a spring at **99** *which travelers were wont to camp. In the morning Major Dade called up Louis and sent him on to Istowatchotka.*

"If you see a black man in the road named Sam, tell him I'll see him—to wait."

Louis went on, but he found no man. He discovered instead the grass mashed down in the woods near the road and concluded that the Indians had been hovering around the camp all that night.

He reported all those things to Major Dade. The major apparently paid little attention to the fears of the guide, for he passed them by and said: "I guess Sam's gone to Wahoo Swamp to keep Christmas."

"No, major. It's worse than 'keep Christmas.' There wasn't a soul on the place."

About that time Major Dade, having decided to send Louis on to Wahoo Swamp, Captain Fraser came up. Said he: "Major, it's dangerous to send this man on. You don't know what the Indians will do."

As Major Dade turned on his heel in disdain, Captain Fraser, turning to the guide, asked:

"What do you think about it, Louis?"

"If the Indians catch me, massa, they'll kill me sure."

Next day Louis didn't go to Wahoo Swamp, but was sent on to reconnoiter. He found fresh tracks in the hammock and told the major that it looked very suspicious.

Major Dade became angry. "Oh," said he, "I'll go through if I have to fly sky-high."

"That same morning," says Louis, "Major Dade said: 'See here, captain, I had a strange dream last night. It was one of the strangest dreams of my life. I dreamed that I was among all the old officers that died in the war.' Then he called them by name and told how each looked, and what they did and what they said."

Some time later the major said: "Louis I have concluded not to send you to Palatkalakashaw today, but I'll send you on to Camp King tomorrow."

"*About this time,*" says Louis, "*I could see that the major was anxious-like. There was a whole 'passel' of hound dogs in the troop, and these were let loose in the woods with men behind them urging them on with a 'Soohy boy! Soohy!'* "

An advance guard was thrown out for the first time the day before the battle, but the advance guard did not precede the troops by more than two hundred yards.

On the morning of the battle the dogs were sent out again but persisted in remaining in the road. They did not hunt through the woods nor bark with any spirit. Louis maintains that the Indians had some strange way of controlling the dogs. One of them said to him a day or two afterwards: "*Don't you think we know what to do to make dogs quiet?*" The guide confessed that he did not, but the red man vouchsafed no further reply than a pitying smile.

After having crossed the Withalacoochee the troops marched for about three miles, at which point there was a broad expanse of open pine-woods, with no other cover than scattered clumps of scrub palmetto and wire grass hardly six inches high. The advance guard was 200 yards ahead of the troops. About a mile up the road Major Dade observed a white mare.

Ordering Louis to come with him he proceeded to investigate, but when half way between the troops and the advance guard, the crack of a rifle was heard close by. Major Dade threw his hand to his breast, cried out, "*My God,*" and fell from his horse with a groan. The shot that killed Major Dade was fired by the head chief of all the Seminoles, Micanopy, and was the signal for the savages to begin the fight.

"*I looked off,*" says Louis, "*and saw the Indians rise up like a string of pepper in a streak of light. They had on only breech-cloths and moccasins. Their bodies were painted red, and when they fired it looked as if lightning had flashed along the whole length of the line. Every man of the advance guard fell. Consternation filled the troops. You could see them waver and tremble. Then the voice of a command rose out and they* remained firm. I thought I had seen the last day of the world. I fell down and laid close down behind a pine tree, beating my head against it and praying. The big gun commenced to speak. The grape-shot tore up the ground all about me. The Indians mocked the gun with derisive yells and 'Puff! Ugh!' and they answered it with bullets which hummed like bees about my ears. All the time the Indians were extending their line. They had a front of nearly a half mile and threw out a wing to the left, all the time converging the two wings and firing from front and flank. They didn't lie down, but stood up and fought like men. The flank movement gave the soldiers so much to do that their attention was drawn for a time from the front. The savages seized the opportunity and advanced rapidly to within one hundred yards, firing with deadly aim. Two Indian boys came up within ten feet of me, jumped back quickly and cocked their guns. One aimed at me but an old Indian knocked the gun barrel up and said: 'Don't kill him.' They passed on by, and three more saw me; but this time the son of Chief Jumper saved me. He said: 'That's a black man. He is not his own master. Don't kill him.' Still another Indian wanted to kill me, but I told him Jumper's son said not to. A moment later this Indian threw his arms in the air and fell dead. One of the bucks who had passed me got a bullet fastened in his gun and ran back. All the Indians saw him run and not knowing what he ran for, followed him.

"This retreat gave the troops a chance to build a breast-work. They set to work with a will and had the trees falling on all sides. They pulled these together but hadn't gotten the stockade more than half completed before the savages found out why one of the braves had run and then they renewed the fight. They left an old crippled colored man to guard me, and he told me that a white man of the Creek (or Cowetha) Indians had been in and out of Tampa and had told the Seminoles that the whites were going to drive them from their homes about Christmas; and that is why the Indians had made the battle.

"Well, the fight kept on until not a single white man was alive. But when they had killed them all, neither the Indians nor the blacks among them stripped the soldiers or hacked and mutilated them. If there was any inclination to do so, it was checked by Chief Jumper, who made a speech to his braves. 'Don't do that,' he said. 'It is bad enough as it is. It will bring us bad luck.' The Indians nor the blacks didn't take a thing from the persons of the soldiers. They all separated and went to their villages. Most of them didn't know there was a single survivor, and when they heard of me they marvelled and came around me in large crowds. They persisted in believing that I knew uncanny arts and had made myself invisible. I told them that I had resorted to no trick, but they didn't believe it.

"The next day I told Jumper that I wanted to go back to my people and that I was Spanish property. He gritted his teeth and said: 'You are enough American for us. Let me tell you, you can't go back. As birds fill the air, so the Seminoles fill the woods.'

"I remained with the Indians for many years and did not go to any of the white settlements until peace was declared. My appearance was the opportunity for the story to be circulated that I had betrayed the troops. They threatened to kill me. When the Indian war broke out again, I was put in irons and sent to Arkansas with the Seminoles, where I lived many years."

The last paragraph of the newspaper story is all that Luis told of his fifty-seven years with the Indians. Most of his movements during that time have never been definitely established but Congressman Giddings believes that he joined the band of a war chief named Wildcat and participated in the attack on Fort Mellon in which eighteen soldiers were killed.

On March 6, 1837, a temporary truce began. Some of the Indians agreed to move to the West, but only on condition that the Negroes who lived with the tribe could go with them. It is almost certain that Luis was present at this council. He was **103**

Wildcat, Seminole war chief and companion of Luis Pacheco. After being removed from Florida to the Indian Territory, Wildcat helped many black slaves escape to freedom in Mexico.

(*Smithsonian Institution*)

under the protection of Chief Jumper, who claimed him as his slave in order to prevent Mrs. Pacheco from taking him back to her plantation.

Luis' owner, as a matter of fact, already was making her first move to reclaim him. General Jesup, fearing that Luis would again escape into the swamps to stir up the remaining Seminoles, shipped him as quickly as possible to New Orleans on his way to the Indian Territory. This move made Mrs.

Pacheco furious, for she had assured the general that she would keep him out of trouble by sending him to her plantation in Cuba.

In New Orleans, Luis almost fell into the hands of slave traders, despite government promises to protect Seminole Negroes from seizure. A trader obtained a court order to hold Luis and thirty-one other black men until it could be determined whether they were recent runaway slaves, rather than free Negroes. But the Army officers refused to surrender them, and in June, 1838, Luis moved on to the Indian Territory.

From that time until his sudden reappearance in Florida more than half a century later little is known of the movements of Luis Pacheco. There is some indication that he worked with Chief Wildcat in protecting Negroes from slave catchers who raided the Indian Territory. In 1850 some of the black men among the Seminoles moved to Mexico to place themselves under the protection of a nation which had abolished slavery. Wildcat and many of his warriors went with them. These Indians and their Negro friends settled just south of the Rio Grande. There they offered refuge to escaping Texas slaves, and in 1852, Wildcat returned to the Indian Territory and assisted a large number of Negroes who were slaves of the Creek Indians to escape to Mexico.

Was Luis with Wildcat in Mexico? He did not say, but Joshua Giddings believed that he was: "Luis Pacheco, with his learning, his shrewdness and tact, was still with Wildcat, the most active and energetic chief of the Seminole Tribe."

While little is known of Luis' activities during this period, much information exists regarding the attempts of Mrs. Pacheco to compel the United States government to repay her for the loss of her valuable slave while employed under Army contract. Claiming Luis to be worth $1,000, she caused a bill to be introduced in Congress in 1847 demanding full payment. An officer who had known Luis testified that it would be better to pay **105** any price for such a man and leave him where he was, or hang him, than to return him to Florida, where some hostile Seminoles still lurked in the swamps.

Joshua Giddings was a member of the House of Representatives at that time, and he played a leading role in the contest which developed between slaveowners and northern Congressmen over Mrs. Pacheco's suit. Tempers flared, and the debate, which had been limited to the merits of the claim, changed to an argument over whether slaves were property to the same extent as horses and cattle. A Congressman from Mississippi brought the debate to a head when he declared "the only question to be that of *property in human flesh*." Giddings instantly leaped to his feet to proclaim that the doctrine of property in human flesh was contrary to "the Declaration of Independence, the Constitution of the United States, to civilization, and to the dictates of our common humanity."

The bill to pay Mrs. Pacheco was passed by a narrow margin in the House of Representatives. Because of the fierce opposition of antislavery members of Congress, however, it was never introduced in the Senate. Giddings commented that "while the gentlemen in the House of Representatives were engaged in discussing the value of Luis Pacheco's bones and sinews, he could probably speak and write more languages with ease and facility than any member of that body."

While the widow Pacheco failed in her campaign to reclaim the slave, Luis was reaching old age in Mexico or Oklahoma, whichever the case may be. At the time of his return to Florida he was ninety-two years old. He died in Jacksonville on January 5, 1895, and was buried at his birthplace. The fact that members of most of the old families of Jacksonville attended his funeral gives some indication they believed his story about the Dade massacre. The newspaper article also caused some historians to change their opinions. Kenneth W. Porter, who had believed absolutely that Luis had plotted to lead

Dade's men into ambush, was much less sure of his ground after reading the interview. He wrote that the reader would have to determine for himself "whether the common belief of Army officers at the time, or the denial of the accused over half a century later," should be believed.

Perhaps Luis provided a made-to-order scapegoat for the Army in attempting to fix the blame for Dade's disastrous defeat.

A LIEUTENANT OF THE BUFFALO SOLDIERS

Henry Ossian Flipper was born into slavery in Thomasville, Georgia, on March 21, 1856. He and his mother belonged to the Reverend Reuben H. Lucky, a Methodist minister. His father, a skilled shoemaker and carriage trimmer named Festus Flipper, belonged to Ephraim G. Ponder, a professional slave trader. In 1859 Ponder moved his slaves to Atlanta, and it appeared that the Flipper family would be broken up. Mrs. Flipper appealed to Ponder to purchase her, but the slave dealer declined. Then both husband and wife appealed to the minister. He was saddened to see them parted, but he could not raise the large price asked for the husband. He was willing, however, to sell the wife. "An agreement was finally made," Henry Flipper stated, "by which the husband paid from his own pocket the purchase-money of his own wife and child, this sum to be returned to him by Mr. Ponder whenever convenient."

In Atlanta one of the slaves who could read and write held school for the Negro children every night in Ponder's woodshop. There, at the age of eight, Henry Flipper received his first instruction. It was an unlikely beginning for a youngster who was to become the first man of his race to be graduated from West Point, a highly successful engineer, an authority on Latin-American affairs, and a high-ranking government official.

During General Sherman's Civil War march through Georgia, Ponder herded his slaves out of Atlanta and fled to Macon. The tread of advancing federal troops sounded the death knell of slavery, however, and in the spring of 1865 Festus Flipper moved his family back to Atlanta as freedmen. There young Henry attended schools provided by the American Missionary Association. With his sights set on a military career, he entered Atlanta University in 1869. Four years later, upon the recommendation of Congressman J. C. Freeman, he was admitted to the United States Military Academy at West Point.

When he entered West Point, Flipper realized that the odds were against him. Other Negro cadets had been admitted, but not one of them had been able to remain for long because of their treatment by white cadets. True enough, slavery had been abolished, but prejudice against Negroes in the Army was as ugly as ever. Military men held to the opinion that Negroes made cowardly soldiers in spite of the fact that black men had served with distinction in almost every major battle in American history.

Henry Flipper wrote a book about his experiences at the academy, *The Colored Cadet at West Point,* in which he described the changes in attitude of his classmates toward him. "When I was a plebe," he wrote, "those of us who lived on the same floor of barracks visited each other, borrowed books, heard each other recite when preparing for examination, and **109**

were really on most intimate terms. But in less than a month they learned to call me 'nigger,' and ceased altogether to visit me. In camp, brought into close contact with old cadets, these once friends discovered that they were prejudiced, and learned to abhor even the presence of a 'd---d' nigger." From that time until graduation no cadet spoke to Flipper except on matters of official business. The officers and instructors treated him with consideration, however, and he avoided trouble by keeping aloof from the cadets. When he was graduated with honors on June 14, 1877, the prejudice disappeared. His fellow graduates offered congratulations and shook hands with him.

During his schooling at West Point, Flipper held to the hope that he would be assigned to the Buffalo Soldiers upon graduation. The Ninth and Tenth Cavalry (Negro troops with white officers) had distinguished themselves in General Phil Sheridan's campaign against Chief Black Kettle's Cheyennes, they had assisted in the rescue of Colonel George A. Forsyth's forces following his heroic defense of Beecher's Island, and they had whipped 500 Comanches at Beaver Creek, Kansas. Flipper was delighted, therefore, when he was commissioned second lieutenant and assigned to the Tenth Cavalry at Fort Sill, Indian Territory.

At Fort Sill the regiment's chief responsibility was to prevent the Indians from raiding into Texas. Shortly after Flipper arrived at the post, Comanches raced their ponies into Fort Sill, cut the cavalry mounts from the picket line, and ran them off

Henry O. Flipper, Lieutenant, 10th U.S. Cavalry. Flipper was the first Negro to graduate from the United States Military Academy at West Point. He fought against Victorio's Apaches, then became a mining engineer, a government official, and an author.

(*Texas Memorial Museum*)

the post in broad daylight. Not long after that, 2,000 Indians came to the fort to demand food for their starving women and children. The braves held a war dance around the flagpole until their demands were met.

In the spring of 1880, Flipper's troop was transferred to Fort Davis, Texas, to help track down the band of Mescalero Apaches led by the fierce old Chief Victorio. The Ninth Cavalry had fought three battles with Victorio's 100 warriors a few months earlier and driven them into Mexico. But undetected by thousands of troops, the Apaches had recrossed the Rio

Company "I," 25th Infantry, in dress uniform, 1883. The 24th and 25th Infantry and the 9th and 10th Cavalry regiments were organized in 1866 to guard the frontier against Indian attack.
(National Archives)

Grande and murdered a stage driver and one of his passengers.

General B. H. Grierson, commanding officer of the Buffalo Soldiers, had laid a trap for Victorio, at Fresno Springs in the Big Bend country of Texas. The troopers looked on in helpless rage while a wagon train blundered into the area, allowing the Apaches to discover the ambush. Next, Victorio had massacred a party of Mexicans, used their bodies as bait, and wiped out a posse which went in search of them.

As soon as Flipper reached Fort Davis, the troop was ordered to move on to abandoned Fort Quitman on the Rio

Squadron of the 9th Cavalry at Ft. Robinson, Nebraska, in 1889. The 9th fought Indians throughout the West. Seven troopers of this regiment won the Congressional Medal of Honor.

(National Archives)

Grande. They set up headquarters at Quitman and sent detachments in various directions to watch for Victorio's raiders. The Apaches surprised one of these patrols 40 miles downriver and made off with their horses and equipment. Two of the troopers, clad only in underclothing, staggered into Fort Quitman to give the alarm. At once Captain Nicholas Nolan, a famous Indian fighter, sent Flipper on a fast horse with a dispatch to General Grierson at Eagle Springs. The young black officer rode 98 **114** miles through a desert crawling with Apaches. As he pulled his

These Yaqui Indians were captured on January 11, 1918, by black cavalrymen during the last Indian fight in United States history. The third figure from the left is an eleven-year-old boy who fired a rifle almost as long as he was tall.

(10th Cavalry and Border Fights by Col. H. B. Wharfield, Ret.)

horse up in front of Grierson's tent, he reeled from the saddle, totally exhausted. But after a few hours' rest he remounted and raced back to Fort Quitman with orders to move Nolan's men to Eagle Springs.

Grierson had only a handful of troops at Eagle Springs, and shortly after Flipper dashed out of camp, the Apaches attacked. Lieutenant Finley and ten black troopers charged the Indians, while Grierson and the rest of his men poured down a withering fire from the rocks. Badly outnumbered, the Buffalo Soldiers stood off the raiders until Flipper made his third ride across the desert, this time at the head of a troop of reinforcements.

"We came in a swinging gallop for fifteen or twenty miles," Flipper noted in his journal which was edited and published after his death by Theodore D. Harris. "When we arrived we found 'G' Troop had already come and the fight was on. We got right into it and soon had the Indians on the run. We lost 19 horses, had two or three men killed, a number wounded.

The 9th and 10th Cavalry saw extensive service in the Indian Territory. Here are black cavalrymen at Medicine Bluff Gap in the heart of hostile Comanche country.

(Field Artillery Museum, Fort Sill, Oklahoma)

And got 19 Indians. I was detailed to read the Episcopal service over them, after which a volley was fired and the buglers sounded taps."

Mauled but still full of fight, Victorio retreated into Mexico, pursued by Buffalo Soldiers, Texas Rangers, and Chiricahua Indian scouts. Below the border, Mexican troops were alerted and it was the army of General Terrazas which caught up with Victorio. A bloody battle raged in the mountains near Tres Castillos. Victorio led a charge on his giant white horse, and the Mexicans riddled him with rifle fire.

As a result of outstanding service while scouting against the Apaches, Flipper was appointed post quartermaster and commissary at Fort Davis and given the responsibility for housing, food, water, fuel, clothing, and equipment. It was a big change for a young man whose experience had all been in the field, and he had some difficulty in keeping his accounts balanced. To add to his problems, some of the officers objected to his taking horseback rides around the post with a white girl. In

Troop "G," 10th Cavalry, crossing a river with Indian prisoners on the way to their post at Tucson, Arizona.

(*National Archives*)

In the Southwest many children were captured by Indians. If taken early enough, they absorbed Indian ways and some of the boys developed into outstanding warriors. This picture, taken in 1886, shows the children of the band of the famous Apache raider Geronimo. Included with the red youngsters are both black and white captives. (N.H. Rose *Collection*)

1881 a new commanding officer, Colonel W. R. Shafter, arrived at Fort Davis. He had a reputation for being hard on young officers, and he took an instant dislike to Flipper.

Shortly after Shafter's assuming command he brought charges of embezzling government funds against Flipper. General Grierson stood by the young officer during his trial, and Flipper was acquitted of the charge. Nevertheless, he was dismissed from the Army for conduct unbecoming an officer.

Flipper was enraged over his dismissal, blaming it on personal dislike and racial prejudice. He made several unsuccessful efforts to reopen the case. Almost twenty years later he laid the matter before General "Fighting Joe" Wheeler, who called it an outrage, but once again nothing was done to reverse the decision.

His military career brought abruptly to an end, Flipper

went to Mexico and became a highly successful civil and mining engineer. William C. Greene, a wealthy investor in mining properties, employed him to search for the legendary lost mine of Tayopa and sent him as far as Spain in quest of clues.

By 1900 the Indian wars in the United States had ended, but hostilities continued south of the border. During his travels through the deserts and mountains of Mexico, Flipper had as many narrow escapes from Indians as he had experienced in his cavalry days. Frequently he found the mutilated bodies of Mexi-

Emblem of the 10th U.S. Cavalry. The Indians had such great respect for the fighting qualities of black troopers that they called them Buffalo Soldiers. The 10th Cavalrymen took pride in the name and wore the buffalo emblem on their uniforms.

(*National Archives*)

cans beside the trail. Once he traveled for three days with a Mexican family, then stopped over in a town for a day while the family went on without him. Father, mother, and children were massacred on the very next morning.

In 1908 Albert B. Fall hired Flipper as a consultant to his Sierra Mining Company. Revolution broke out in Mexico, and in 1912 all of the company's employees were moved to safety at El Paso, Texas. Flipper had become an authority on Mexican politics, and Fall, then a United States Senator, called on him for information which was presented to the Congressional Subcommittee on Latin-American Affairs.

This report was only the beginning of Flipper's work for the government. In 1919 Senator Fall summoned him to Washington to serve as Spanish interpreter. Two years later, Fall was appointed Secretary of the Interior. One of his first acts was to appoint as his assistant the black man who had been dismissed from the Army as unfit to serve.

Flipper held the important position of Assistant Secretary of the Interior until 1923. Then he returned to Latin America as a consultant to oil companies. In 1931 he retired to live in Atlanta with his brother, Joseph S. Flipper, a bishop of the African Methodist Episcopal Church.

Flipper's last years were spent in writing articles for newspapers and magazines about the history of Mexico and the Southwest. One of his publications was a booklet entitled *Did a Negro Discover Arizona and New Mexico?* Four centuries after the death of Estevanico, the first Negro known to American history, an account of his exploits was written by the last of the black frontiersmen. Thus the saga of Negroes and Indians had come full cycle—and with it the sordid story of slavery—for Estevanico, the African, had been born into freedom and enslaved in a Spanish invasion, while Flipper, the American, had been born into slavery and freed in a federal

invasion.

BIBLIOGRAPHY

ABEL, ANNIE HELOISE, *The American Indian as Slaveholder and Secessionist.* Cleveland, Arthur H. Clark, 1915.

American State Papers: Indian Affairs. Washington, Gales and Seaton, 1832.

BAKELESS, JOHN, *Daniel Boone.* New York, Morrow, 1939.

———, *Lewis and Clark.* New York, Morrow, 1947.

BECKWOURTH, JAMES P., *Life and Adventures of James P. Beckwourth.* New York, Knopf, 1931.

BISHOP, MORRIS, *The Odyssey of Cabeza de Vaca.* New York, Century, 1933.

BOLTON, HERBERT, *The Spanish Borderlands.* New Haven, Yale University Press, 1921.

BOYD, MARK F., *Florida Aflame.* Tallahassee, Florida Board of Parks and Historic Memorials, 1951.

CHITTENDEN, HIRAM MARTIN, *The American Fur Trade of the Far West.* New York, Press of the Pioneers, 1935.

CLELAND, ROBERT GLASS, *This Reckless Breed of Men.* New York, Knopf, 1950.

CRANE, VERNER W., *The Southern Frontier. 1670–1732,* Chapel Hill, N. C., Duke University Press, 1928.

DALE, HARRISON CLIFFORD, *The Ashley-Smith Explorations.* Glendale, Calif., Arthur H. Clark, 1941.

DESHIELDS, JAMES T., *Border Wars of Texas.* Tioga, Texas, Herald Company, 1912.

DICKINSON, JONATHAN, *Jonathan Dickinson's Journal.* New Haven, Yale University Press, 1945.

Draper Manuscripts (unpublished), MMS 4C, 11C, 16C18.

DUNN, J. P., *Massacres of the Mountains.* New York, Harper, 1886.

DUNHAM, PHILIP, AND JONES, EVERETT L., *The Negro Cowboys.* New York, Dodd, Mead, 1965.

FILSON, JOHN, *The Discovery and Settlement of Kentucke.* Wilmington, Del., printed by James Adams, 1784.

FINLEY, JAMES B., *Life Among the Indians.* Cincinnati, printed at the Methodist Book Concern for the author, 1857.

FLIPPER, HENRY OSSIAN, *The Colored Cadet at West Point.* New York, H. Lee, 1878.

————, *The Negro Frontiersman.* El Paso, Texas Western College Press, 1963.

Florida Times-Union. October 30, 1892, January 8, 1895.

GARRARD, LEWIS H., *Wah-To-Yah and the Taos Trail.* Glendale, Calif., Arthur H. Clark, 1938.

GIDDINGS, JOSHUA, *The Exiles of Florida.* Columbus, Ohio, Follett, 1858.

HAMMON, BRITON, *A Narrative of the Uncommon Sufferings and Surprizing Deliverance of Briton Hammon, a Negro Man.* Boston, Greene & Russell, 1760.

HERSKOVITS, MELVILLE J., *The American Negro, a Study in Racial Crossing.* New York, Knopf, 1928.

HODGE, FREDERICK WEBB, *Handbook of American Indians North of Mexico.* Washington, Government Printing Office, 1912.

HOLMES, REUBEN, "The Five Scalps." *Glimpses of the Past.* V (1938).

IRVING, WASHINGTON, *Astoria.* New York, Putnam, 1849.

JACKSON, DONALD, *Letters of the Lewis and Clark Expedition.* Urbana, University of Illinois Press, 1962.

JELTZ, WYATT F., "Negroes and Choctaw and Chickasaw Indians." *Journal of Negro History.* XXXIII (1948).

KATZ, WILLIAM LOREN, *Eyewitness, the Negro in American History.* New York, Pitman, 1967.

LECKIE, WILLIAM H., *The Buffalo Soldiers.* Norman, University of Oklahoma Press, 1967.

LEONARD, ZENAS, *Adventures of Zenas Leonard.* Chicago, Lakeside Press, 1934.

LOWERY, WOODBURY, *The Spanish Settlements Within the Present Limits of the United States, 1513–1561.* New York, Putnam's, 1901.

MCREYNOLDS, EDWIN C., *The Seminoles.* Norman, University of Oklahoma Press, 1957.

MARCY, RANDOLPH B., *Thirty Years of Army Life on the Border.* Philadelphia, Lippincott, 1963.

MARRANT, JOHN, *A Narrative of the Life of John Marrant.* Leeds, printed by Davies and Co., 1810.

MITCHELL, JOSEPH, *The Missionary Pioneer.* New York, J. C. Totten, 1827.

MORGAN, DALE L., *Jedediah Smith and the Opening of the West.* Indianapolis, Bobbs-Merrill, 1953.

MUMEY, NOLIE, *James Pierson Beckwourth, 1856–1866.* Denver, Rosenstock, 1957.

MYERS, JOHN, *Pirate, Pawnee and Mountain Man.* Boston, Little, Brown, 1963.

NIZA, MARCOS DE, *The Journey of Fray Marcos de Niza.* Dallas, University Press in Dallas, 1949.

NUNEZ CABEZA DE VACA, Àlvar, *The Journey of Àlvar Núñez Cabeza de Vaca.* Chicago, Rio Grande Press, 1964.

PARKMAN, FRANCIS, *The Oregon Trail.* New York, Macmillan, 1930.

PICKETT, ALBERT JAMES, *History of Alabama and Incidentally of Georgia and Mississippi.* Sheffield, Ala., R. C. Randolph, 1896.

PORTER, KENNETH W., "The Early Life of Luis Pacheco ne Fatio," *The Negro History Bulletin.* VII (1943).

————, "Indians and Negroes on the Texas Frontier," *Journal of Negro History.* XLI (1956).

————, "Negroes on the Southern Frontier," *Journal of Negro History.* XXXIII (1948).

————, "Relations Between Negroes and Indians," *Journal of Negro History.* XVII (1932).

POTTER, WOODBURNE, *The War in Florida.* Baltimore, Lewis and Coleman, 1836.

REDDICK, L. D., "Negro Policy in the United States Army," *Journal of Negro History.* XXXIV (1949).

RICHARDSON, RUPERT NORVAL, *The Comanche Barrier to South Plains Settlement.* Glendale, Calif., Arthur H. Clark, 1933.

RICKEY, DON, JR., *Forty Miles a Day on Beans and Hay.* Norman, University of Oklahoma Press, 1963.

RISTER, CARL COKE, *The Southwestern Frontier.* Cleveland, Arthur H. Clark, 1928.

STARKEY, MARION L., *The Cherokee Nation.* New York, Knopf, 1946.

SWANTON, JOHN R., *The Indians of the Southeastern United States.* Washington, Government Printing Office, 1946.

THWAITES, REUBEN GOLD, *Original Journals of the Lewis and Clark Expedition.* New York, Antiquarian Press, 1959.

VAIL, R. W. G., *The Voice of the Old Frontier.* Philadelphia, University of Pennsylvania Press, 1949.

WELLMAN, PAUL I., *Death on Horseback.* Philadelphia, Lippincott, 1947.

WHARFIELD, H. B., *10th Cavalry & Border Fights.* El Cajon, Calif., 1965.

WILBARGER, J. W., *Indian Depredations in Texas.* Austin, Texas, Steck, 1935.

WILLIAMS, JOHN, *The Redeemed Captive Returning to Zion.* Northampton, Mass., Hopkins, Bridgman, and Co., 1853.

WILLIAMS, JOHN LEE, *The Territory of Florida.* Gainesville, University of Florida Press, 1962.

WILLSON, MINNIE MOORE, *The Seminoles of Florida.* New York, Moffat, Yard and Co., 1920.

WOOD, WILLIAM, *New England's Prospect.* Boston, reprinted by E. M. Boynton, 1898.

INDEX

125

127